HR MADE SIMPLE

D0988609

Recruit. Engage. Comply.
It's that Easy!

AMANDA KING, SPHR

Amanda King, Operam HR
257 E. Market St, 2nd floor
York, PA 17403

 Year of the Book
135 Glen Ave.
Glen Rock, PA 17327

ISBN 10: 1-945670-31-2
ISBN 13: 978-1-945670-31-2

Dedication

This isn't how I thought my life would turn out. I never thought I'd be a human resources professional. I never thought I'd end up living in the town I grew up in. And I never thought I'd be an entrepreneur.

But isn't that life?

I was fortunate to have followed a path that's led me to great things and I've had great people along the way to help. In both phases of my professional life – the corporate and the entrepreneurial – I took the lead from others and it helped me become successful quickly.

Special thanks to my family and friends for always being there to support me with all phases of my life. Deep gratitude to my first manager and life-long mentor, Nick Nicholson, without whom I wouldn't be where I am today both personally and professionally. And to all the leaders, colleagues, team members, and connections I've made along the way – thank you for teaching me new things and keeping me on track!

This book is designed to help you take on challenges in your business you might not be comfortable handling – people. Interpersonal relationships in the workplace become ever more personal when it's your own business. It's hard to stay agnostic to the actions of others when it's your business and your money. For the entrepreneur, everything you do is personal in many ways. I hope this book will help you create a process for the people-aspects of your business so you can approach this part of your growth plan with objectivity and proper direction. And maybe I can be one of those in your network who can teach you something and keep you on track too!

All the best,

Amanda

Table of Contents

Introduction

Dealing with the fear of hiring

I always thought I would work for a corporation, and then I would work for progressively bigger corporations until I became the VP of Global Human Resources. That's exactly what I thought I was going to do.

As it turned out, that's not what I was *destined* to do.

The career path I thought was going to be *killer perfect* for me was something I was not suited for at all.

Perhaps you've felt this way, too. But why?

In my pursuit of all things corporate I sought yet another assignment at yet another large company. I took a personality assessment as part of the selection process. I felt good. I mean, I was confident that I'd impressed the interviewers and was a clear match for the company's needs.

A few days after the interview and assessment the industrial psychologist called me and said, "I'm not going to recommend you for this job."

Um... what?! Doesn't he know this is exactly what I set out to do in my life? What's wrong with him?

This was a life changing event for me, but not just because I heard news I wasn't prepared to hear. Not just because I wasn't going to get something I wanted. This conversation ultimately set me down the path I should be walking. And it happened in a big way.

It turns out that what I *am* suited for is to be an entrepreneur. But starting a business was not anything I'd ever done before.

It was not something I was trained to do. It was simply an outgrowth of what I was already passionate about.

Perhaps you've discovered that entrepreneurial drive as well. Your talent, your skills, and your passion are what motivate you to succeed. You want to serve. And you want to show up in a big way.

But now that your business is growing – going better than you ever could have imagined – you're facing worries like, "What do I do now?" and "How do I scale this thing?"

"I can't keep staying up until 1:00 A.M., living my dream. I'm exhausted!"

You created a business because you followed your dreams. You have the best product idea or service the market needs. You are good at what you do.

Then your idea grew. Your business flourished. You started hiring employees. You rented a bigger office. Things were going great!

But about those employees. They take a lot of time and energy... and money. Supporting your employees takes you away from your dream, the work that you're good at doing, and the support you need to give to your customers.

Sometimes employees don't show up to work. They don't have the same passion for the business that you do. They cost a lot of money and are never grateful for what you do for them!

This can feel like a one-sided relationship between you and the people you have hired to help make your dream a success.

I understand these fears. I reached a place in my own business growth where I could not keep up. The market had proven my business concept was sound, and then it was time to grow beyond my one-woman storefront. I needed to hire people.

If I hadn't taken this step, I would've sabotaged my business. If I didn't take the step to find someone else to complement my skills, or if I didn't find a group of capable individuals, I wouldn't be able to help many more clients. All I would have been was a struggling entrepreneur.

The harsh reality

It's really hard to counsel yourself. You need advice on how to get through the steps of hiring team members – whether that means the freelance route, sub-contractors, or direct employment.

Even though I have helped countless companies and managers hire people for their team, there is fear when I hire people for my own business.

When you work for another corporation the decisions are easier to make. When people are working for you, it's personal. You may know what has to be done. You may know how to go out to the marketplace and find the best people. But you also need to know how to get all the employee tax forms done, how to submit documents to the state government, and how to set up payroll and onboard your new employees, and help set up their employment goals and objectives.

And... you need to know how to make it work in *your* company.

The fear and "What If" monsters sing in your head, *"What if this person steals my ideas? What if this person doesn't work very hard? What if this person does all the things that every hiring manager has warned me about?"*

The "What If" monsters could have sabotaged my business. And they might be sabotaging yours. This book is my way of giving back to you the method I used to grow my own business and the advice I give to successful clients with regard to the employees on their teams.

> *"I know of no single formula for success. But over the years I have observed that some attributes of leadership are universal and are often about finding ways of encouraging people to combine their efforts, their talents, their insights, their enthusiasm and their inspiration to work together."*
> ~Queen Elizabeth II

You want to make sure you are looking for the right talent for your business. What do you need right now? What do you need in the near future?

Please don't get caught up thinking, "Five years from now, I want the company to look like this," because you will constantly be second-guessing yourself. You're never going to find someone to join your team who can achieve that goal for you. *You* don't even know what that goal looks like right now. How can someone else possibly manage that?

When you first get started in the hiring process for your company, think about more immediate needs in the shorter term for your business, and then it won't feel so tough to bring the right person on board. You can add future growth and goals into your hiring strategy in the future.

There are many tools available to help you find talent. Some of them cost a lot of money, while others are pretty simple. This book will give you a combination of both so you can pick and choose what you need to optimize your situation... and your future business growth.

Challenge yourself to think differently about the talent you bring into your organization, and about how you're going to recruit that talent. Will an employee work part-time or full-time? Temporary hire or through a contracted third party? And how will that employee be compensated?

Now, imagine how you would want to be compensated if you were that person. Really, put yourself in their shoes. What would make this opportunity most appealing for them?

It doesn't always mean earning $100k with profit sharing and a 401(k) plan. Quite frankly, you probably can't afford to offer that right now anyway.

Whatever team profile you choose, the tools you use to hire are pretty much the same.

Don't over-think it. Simply put yourself in the shoes of someone who's thinking about joining your one-, or two-, or 500-person firm (depending on where you are right now), and create a package that makes sense for all of you.

As an entrepreneur, when you don't have ample human resources to sustain growth, you're sabotaging your business – the exact opposite of what you most desire.

Borrow tactics from other areas of your business like finance, sales, and operations. These departments have a structure, a set of processes, and a level of expectation for delivery back to the business. The management of your team – your *human resources* – should have the same systematic approach. Failure to implement processes and systems will cripple your business.

If you have decided to pick up this book, the truth is that a lack of systems is probably crippling your business right now.

Within these pages I'll teach you how to bring employees into your company who will help you flourish, wherever you are right now. Then you'll learn how to create an environment that maintains, sustains, and retains that wonderful talent resource. Finally, I'll give you all the tools you need to make sure your business is compliant with employment rules and regulations.

Establishing systems and setting expectations will help you find the best talent, retain your key team members, and keep you out of hot water with issues of non-compliance.

This book is a guide to de-mystify employment processes, help you establish good practices for your business, and let you focus more of your time on the dream that caused you to create your business in the first place.

It's time to stop sabotaging your business... like everyone else.

RECRUIT

Finding Talent

The Prep Work

Why did you start this company?
What are the values and priorities of your business?

Think back to when you started your company. What was the driving force behind your decision? Maybe you wanted to create an innovative product that would completely disrupt the market. Maybe you saw an opportunity to provide a service to other companies.

When is the last time you thought back to that initial, creative spark that lit the way for you to build your business?

Reflecting on your values and priorities is an essential part of your business's success. From a prep-work standpoint, it's important to articulate those ideas to your current staff and the talent you recruit into your business. The reasons you created your business, and the direction in which you want it to proceed, set the tone and culture of your company. If you don't say those things out loud and don't include all staff in your external communications, then no one knows your voice.

The first prep work for you to do is to define the values you want for your business, and the priorities your team members should have.

ACTION – Outline values

What's the reason you started your company?

_____

_____

_____

Where are you today at fulfilling that original dream?

_____

_____

_____

If your original dream has changed in the years you've been in business, how is it different?

_____

_____

_____

What are some of the key words or phrases you think about when you think of *value*? (EX: Innovation, Success, Differentiation, Domination)

_____

_____

_____

ACTION – Outline priorities

What are the goals you have for the business in the next year?

_____

_____

_____

What are the goals you have for the business in the next 5 years?

_____

_____

_____

What path are you heading down to meet these goals?

_____

_____

_____

What's the #1 priority you have for your business right now?

_____

_____

_____

For a more detailed worksheet on these topics, visit:
OperamHR.com/book
Click on the HIRE section, and enter code: SimpleHR

Now that you've outlined your values and goals, how do you use that information to find the best talent?

Employees learn about you and your company before they're employees. It happens even before they are candidates. People might get to know your company as customers, visitors, or through your network. They get an impression of you even before employment is a topic.

It's easier to understand this concept when you think about other parts of your company. As you develop sales and marketing strategies for your business, you know you have to think about messaging, consistency, and targeting an audience. The talent pipeline works the same way – both before and after employment begins.

Let's break it down into pieces.

How do you find candidates to join your company? Are there certain websites that lead to the best recruiting? Are there printed publications or industry associations which have brought talented people to your team?

If that's the case – what does your company profile look like to an outsider who visits those sites?

Log in to those sites right now and check the links and verbiage about your company. If it's outdated – update it now. Go ahead and do this right now, because there's no time like the present!

I'll wait for you until you get done...

You're back?!? Okay – good. Now let's focus on the impression of your business.

When you look at your company's website, what is the first thing a candidate will learn about your company?

If you aren't ready to update your entire website, maybe you should consider creating a landing page just for employment purposes. It can mirror your company page but should be geared to telling the employment story of your company, its culture, and what makes employees successful at your business. It could also capture information on potential candidates (name, email, current job title) for future reference in your recruiting endeavors.

Landing pages are a much easier way to communicate employment messages to candidates. Not familiar with a landing page? Think of it as a complement to your existing website, but the beauty of a landing page is that you don't have to completely revamp your existing website. The landing page can include only the information you need – in this case, employment brand or application process – without replicating the customer or service/product-specific items on your website. Landing pages are generally easy to create and maintain. You could also work with a local web developer or inexpensive contractor on sites like Fiverr.com or Upwork.com.

For a more detailed worksheet on your recruiting strategy, visit:
OperamHR.com/book
Click on the HIRE section, and enter code: SimpleHR

Let's talk about you

What impression would a candidate get if they did some research on you? If you haven't done a Google search or LinkedIn search for your personal profile, you should do that very soon. It's incredible the information that's out there about each and every one of us.

You have some control over this information – though sadly you can't control every piece of data.

Start with the sites you *can* control: LinkedIn, Glassdoor, and your Google Business page. Make sure the information is up-to-date and relevant for your business and professional profiles.

You may be able to modify or delete some comments or posts so your brand is represented honestly and fairly. If there are posts from people you can't modify or delete, that's okay – read them, print them, commit them to memory. This feedback is in the public domain for better or worse. Your responsibility is to consider that information and make changes to your brand if it's not reflecting the right image.

Why is this step important?

Regardless if you're the business owner or you are a member of the company's management team, a savvy candidate is going to be interested in learning about your background. A candidate might investigate it as part of her job prospecting, who's in her network, or in interview preparations. Your profile is important as are the profiles of others in your company. Think about asking team members to update their profiles as well. I think this is particularly important if you have a small company with low general recognition in the community. The more people who are connected to your company with their backgrounds highlighted online, the stronger impression it will give to top talent in the candidate pool.

Oh – and one other thing – this is FREE for you to do!

Let's go inside your company

Is your team prepared to be your recruitment advocacy group?

Your staff knows more about your business than perhaps even you! They're a great resource to send realistic messages to employment candidates. Your current team will be the best advocates to bring in people with whom they want to work and who will make the team stronger.

However, in order for them to be the best advocates for your company's recruiting efforts, there is some information with which they need to be armed. Here's a starting list for you to consider:

- Do your team members understand the financial health or growth vision of the company?
- Do your team members know who's been promoted in the last year?
- Do your team members know how you view their performance and contributions to the business so they can share it with others?
- Do your team members have online profiles that show their employment with your company, their title, and a description of the work they do?

These questions will help you think about the employee's view of the employment experience at your company. I like to call this the "employment life cycle" and sometimes I refer to it as the employee value proposition. It doesn't matter what you call it. It matters if you're putting thought and action into it.

Online Profile Guide

Check your personal and company profiles on:

- ☐ LinkedIn
- ☐ Glassdoor
- ☐ Facebook
- ☐ Twitter
- ☐ Instagram
- ☐ Google / G+

What needs to be updated on each site?

- ☐ Your name
- ☐ Your company
- ☐ Your title
- ☐ Description of the work you do
- ☐ Achievements in your career
- ☐ Professional photo

Share this listing with other team members so they can check their profiles as well. Maybe even consider preparing for them a company summary to use for the company. For example:

> As the experts in business communications services for engineering and construction firms, Top Notch Technologies has been delivering innovative solutions to customers for forty years. Our award-winning technology enables companies worldwide to gain real-time data visibility that drives productivity. We deliver innovative products that are tailored to our customer's needs. With headquarters in Chicago, Illinois, the company supports businesses worldwide. See our successes at *www.TopNotchTech.com*.

Where Do I Start?

When you're thinking about bringing individuals into your company – a freelancer, contractor, temp, full-time employee, or business partner – I think you have to first establish what it is you really need. Then you're ready to answer why you would hire someone and what certain type of business relationship that should entail.

Before creating a candidate profile, it's important for you to outline who you are as a leader. Whether you own the business or you work in someone else's business, you really have to identify some of your own strengths and weaknesses. (I know I'm supposed to say "opportunities" rather than "weaknesses" – but honestly, we all have strengths and weaknesses. That's just the way that it is.) You need to outline some of those things, because the best hire you're going to make should complement the skills you are best at doing, and fill in the blanks for the ones for which you are the worst.

You should definitely take time to do this first step. I'm not talking about some sort of psycho analysis, blah, blah, blah, I'm talking about knowing what you personally do well. Who do you need to bring in to complement those skill sets? Or to do the things you hate that currently get in the way of you growing your business?

I prefer sales and marketing to writing employee handbooks, even though I write a lot of them, and I'm pretty good at doing it. But when I ask myself 'Who do I need to complement my own skills,' I realize it would be better to have someone with stronger HR competencies than a sales and marketing professional.

This is why I'm asking you to think about what would be the best use of *your* time. For each of the tasks in your business, think about the traits in a candidate's past experience that would result in success in your business. What does that candidate's profile look like, and how can you target that individual in the marketplace?

Let's say for example, you've been spending a lot of time doing administrative work. Before you go out and hire a high-powered salesperson or an account representative or even a customer service person, wouldn't it make more sense to offload some of that administrative work? You could bring on a freelancer or contract position to handle some of those administrative tasks, and free yourself up to tackle jobs you prefer.

If financial transactions are not your strong suit, maybe you need to partner with someone who can provide that valuable advice. One way entrepreneurs and business owners sabotage their companies over and over again is by not knowing their numbers. I credit Marcus Lemonis of CNBC's *The Profit* for teaching me that. If you are not the best at this critical skill, then maybe you need to contract a CPA or a third-party billing firm to take care of those financial aspects. Alternatively, this person could run some financial analysis for you as a guide to what you can afford to hire in terms of employees or contractors.

When creating a candidate profile, remember to look at your own skill set, your own abilities, and your own personality. Personality is one of the toughest things to interview for, but it's something that can inevitably make you frustrated with a new hire. And chances are, it will also make that new employee frustrated enough to leave.

You're in it for the long haul, right? You're the manager, you're the owner, you are the leader of the organization. You're staying. And your new employee(s) will be staying until they don't want to be there anymore... or until you can find a valid reason for them to not be there.

You also want to hire an individual who complements your other team members. Personality is often the conflict individuals point to as a reason they want to leave an organization. I frequently hear that employees don't leave companies, they leave their supervisors and managers.

Take time to think about your management style and what you're willing to tolerate before you go into the marketplace to hire someone. If you can't clearly communicate your expectations and what type of personality, skill set, and experience you want in a team member, you're going to get all kinds of applicants. And then you'll sit through interviews saying, "My God, none of these people match anything I want. What a waste of my time."

Don't let this happen to you because you didn't do your homework up front. Instead, spend a few minutes thinking about your business and management profile before you go out into the marketplace.

Job descriptions versus postings

Writing a job posting is somewhat different than writing a job description. Job descriptions are a compliance tool and job postings are a marketing tool. One is internal and the other is external. I'll cover more on job descriptions in the Compliance section.

In reality you should write the job description first because the job description outlines the work required.

For the job posting tool, visit: OperamHR.com/book
Click on the HIRE section and enter code: SimpleHR
Look for Job Posting Worksheet

How do you write an effective job posting?

Just like your business marketing targets specific customers, job postings should communicate with a targeted candidate pool.

I'll address how to target specific candidates soon, but let's start with work you've already done.

The first part of a job posting needs to communicate information about your business to candidates. Just like your customers – especially "cold" customers who aren't already warmed up to your business – you need to give a description of the company and explain *why* someone would want to work for you.

Using keywords from your values and priorities statement, write a narrative that will appear in *every single job posting* you place online or in print.

Here's an example, from a company called Top Notch Technologies:

> As the experts in business communications services for engineering and construction firms, Top Notch Technologies has been delivering innovative solutions to customers for forty years. Our award-winning technology enables companies worldwide to gain real-time data visibility that drives productivity. We deliver innovative products that are tailored to our customer's needs. With headquarters in Chicago, Illinois, the company supports businesses worldwide. See our successes at: www.TopNotchTech.com.

It's your turn. Write a basic introduction of your company here:

_____

_____

_____

_____

_____

_____

_____

_____

_____

_____

_____

_____

_____

_____

_____

The next thing to communicate is what experience a candidate will need to be successful at your company. One approach you can take is to copy and paste the bullets from your job description. That's what most companies do when they post a job.

You're going to be different.

The way to attract the best talent for your company is to present to candidates *what's in it for them*, not what's in it for you. You need to communicate these things:

- How can someone be successful at your company?
- What past experiences would help make someone successful in the open position at your company?
- What types of values or behaviors are encouraged at your company?
- What skills can someone develop by working at your company?
- What benefits do you offer people who work on your team?

Here is an example of what the posting looks like for Top Notch Tech:

Who is Top Notch Technologies?

As the experts in business communications services for engineering and construction firms, Top Notch Technologies has been delivering innovative solutions to customers for forty years. Our award-winning technology enables companies worldwide to gain real-time data visibility that drives productivity. We deliver innovative products that are tailored to our customer's needs. With headquarters in Chicago, Illinois, the company supports businesses worldwide. See our successes at www.TopNotchTech.com.

The opportunity for you

Top Notch Technologies has an opportunity for an Accountant to join its Houston, TX location. Our success is based on our employees working as a team in every aspect of the business. Our finance team supports each of our company's profit centers by working closely with other department leaders like sales, operations, IT, and customer support. Each person is a partner and a team member – whether it's working on projects, special assignments or your very important "day job"!

Your career

A successful accounting career at Top Notch Technologies will have the opportunity to partner with other departments through project participation and project management. The career path for this team includes taking on successively challenging roles on the finance team as well as cross-functional project teams and opportunities to transfer to other departments to broaden your skills.

The opportunity

To be successful in the current opening as an accountant requires someone who is a great communicator, team player, someone who feels confident voicing his/her opinion on the right decisions for the business and someone who has the following experiences:

Monthly account reconciliation

Using an ERP or similar accounting system on a daily basis

Create reports and performs analysis on the data

Post entries and make necessary corrections to the general ledger (GL)

Proficient knowledge in the Microsoft Suite like Excel, Word, PowerPoint and Outlook

Bachelor's Degree (BA or BS) in accounting, finance, or general business from an accredited 4-year institution

Minimum of 4 years' experience with general accounting practices

Prefer someone who has achieved the CPA accreditation or who has started the process toward achieving the CPA

The benefits

Top Notch Technologies offers employees a competitive portfolio of benefits like medical, dental, and vision insurance; the opportunity to participate in health savings accounts (HSA) and flexible spending accounts (FSA); employer-paid life insurance; 4 weeks of paid time off and annual bonus eligibility.

Job Profile Guide

Instructions

Think about how someone can be successful in this position.

Does this position require someone who likes to work alone or on a team?

_____

_____

Does the position need someone who is just starting a career or someone who has experience?

_____

_____

Is it someone who has unique skills? List them.

_____

_____

_____

Is it someone who has certain management skills like project management, personnel management, budget management, etc.?

_____

What does your company do?

Write a summary of the services, products or technology that your company provides; what industry; typical clients; where you have locations; and where this position would be based.

_____

_____

_____

_____

_____

What does your business do and what industries do you support?

_____

_____

_____

_____

What is the opportunity for a candidate who joins your team?

_____

_____

_____

Value proposition

Think about why someone would join your company. Why is working for your company a good thing for a candidate?

Here are some examples:

- ☐ Leader in your industry
- ☐ Exciting technology
- ☐ Progressive benefits package
- ☐ Flexible work schedules
- ☐ Awesome work environment
- ☐ Is this a career advancement for someone? State why.
- ☐ Does your company offer medical or financial benefits?

_____

_____

_____

_____

For a more detailed worksheet on these topics including outlining the Essential Skills, Education, and Behaviors for your job posting, visit:

OperamHR.com/book

Click on the HIRE section and enter code: SimpleHR

Look for Job Posting Worksheet

How Do You Find Rock Star Talent?

Finding the best staff for your company may be one of the greatest frustrations you'll have as a business owner or manager. You may post jobs online and get bombarded with candidates who aren't even remotely qualified. Then you finally get through the interview process and hire one of them.

Why is it that the most promising candidates often become the worst employees?

Just as in other facets of your business, establishing a tried-and-true process for hiring will help you obtain more reliable results. For example, you probably don't make changes to your supply chain without some thought about how it will financially impact your business. It's also doubtful you throw money at sales and marketing without thinking about a return on your investment. In the exact same way, you should have a game plan for recruiting and hiring top talent at your company, too.

Here are some tips:

1. Build a brand

You want your customers to see your business in a certain image. Make sure your employment candidates see you in that same positive, consistent image.

Use your company's LinkedIn profile as a way to highlight your team members' accomplishments. Ask your staff to write content for your LinkedIn page, website, or Twitter feed. The more your team writes, the more honest the content will seem to prospective candidates. If you show that your team is already made up of rock stars, you're more likely to attract additional rock stars to join you.

Check out what PepsiCo.com does with its "People of PepsiCo" page:

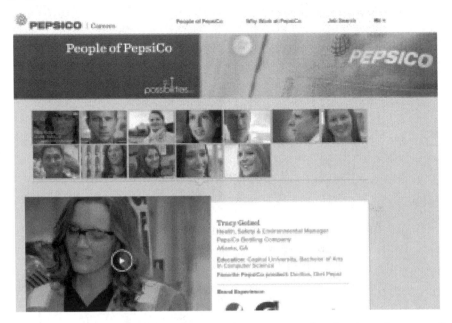

PepsiCo helps candidates see inside the company by sharing photos and videos of current associates in their working environment doing their daily jobs.

Earlier I mentioned creating a landing page for your recruiting efforts. This allows you to feature all your company's jobs which are posted, without the need for an entire website rebuild. Well, if you've create a landing page for your recruiting efforts, that's where you can also house most of the information you'll read in the next 7 steps. And remember, Fiverr.com or Upwork.com and other contractor sites can easily create and update these types of tools for you!

2. Be seen

If you were a prospective employment candidate for your own company, where would you look for a job listing?

Post your job listings on the sites which are most likely to target your best candidates. Are there key organizations for your specific industry? Are there professional organizations where top talent would hold membership? If so, find out if you can advertise on their website or trade publications. Websites are typically less expensive than print, but depending on the demographic you're targeting, you might want to consider both avenues.

3. Be specific

You are looking for top talent, but it still has to be talent who can perform the work and fit into your culture.

Be specific about the job needs so a candidate can determine if she's a fit before applying. Job postings typically go into detail about skills and experience, but what about other facets of working at your company?

Think about work environment. If you have an open-air workspace with no walls, no offices, and very few private areas, then you should mention this in your job posting. Or embed a photo in the posting because people are visual. For example, WeWork is a global corporation which provides co-working space. Check out their photos and videos of Brooklyn Heights office space:

4. Be inviting

If you're having a dinner party, what's the best way to make sure your guests attend? Great invitations, polite correspondence and the promise of a good time for your guests!

When you are corresponding with job candidates via email, voicemail, or live video, remember that the prospective employee is gaining an impression of you as much as you are of them. It's a good idea to be polite, respectful of their time, and courteous in your responses. Offer information about the company, location, or department even if the person doesn't ask. It will help them feel like you're being welcoming and going above and beyond your competition!

5. Be sure to reply

When a candidate applies, respond to their application. It can be as simple as, "Thank you for applying! I am receiving many applications right now but hope to connect with you within two weeks."

If you don't send a response, the candidate is likely to think that a) you're not interested; b) you don't really care that they've applied; or c) you're rude. YIKES!

Following the interview, if the candidate sends a thank you note via email, it's courteous to respond in acknowledgment. (I bet your competition isn't doing that!)

6. Be responsive

The best candidates ask questions. Respond to those questions. Better yet – anticipate them by having a pro-active contact process. Remember each candidate may be submitting resumes to 10-15 companies at one time during their search. You need to differentiate your company from the competition. Having quick response time is a good tactic. An even better tactic is to send candidates information about your company via an auto-email process. You can include things like pictures of the workplace, industry statistics, links to awards won by your company or employees, or a listing to a stock profile if you're a publicly traded organization. Set it up once and it will do the work for you!

7. Be prepared

Candidates want to know what advantages there are to joining your company. Be prepared with job descriptions, benefits summaries, and a compensation overview. If you create interest in your company with the candidate and lay out an offer they can't refuse, you're going to land the best people to fill those openings.

8. Be honest

Show candidates who your company is, what it stands for, and what kind of culture you've created. Go beyond pointing to the corporate mission statement that's pinned to the wall in the cafeteria or breakroom. Candidates want to hear you emulating those ideas – otherwise it seems like baseless 'corporate speak'.

There are challenges at every company, and while you don't want to share your deepest darkest secrets in the job interview, it's important to be truthful with someone. If you expect them to work 9-10 hour days at the beginning of their employment, you should tell them that. Don't be fearful of this! If you're not honest at the interview stage and you hire someone who wants no more than 8-hour work days, you're both going to be disappointed very quickly!

For a more detailed worksheet on these topics including outlining the Essential Skills, Education, and Behaviors for your job posting, visit OperamHR.com/book

Click on the HIRE section and enter code: SimpleHR
Look for Job Posting Worksheet

Top Talent Isn't in One Place

I bet you have an incredible marketing and sales strategy for your business. After all, you're in it for revenue and profit, right?

I bet you hired market researchers to determine the best channels and segments to focus product development, marketing and sales efforts. After all, if the products or services don't sell, you aren't going to be in business long, right?

So what's your plan for recruiting top talent?

Hmm.... if you hear crickets chirping, you're not alone. Most companies do not have a strategy for finding top talent. They don't have a plan for hiring mediocre talent either, so don't count yourself alone in this predicament.

Tapping into one customer pool will not yield the best sales, right? So why are you tapping into just one talent pool to find the best staff for your company? You need a combination of avenues to make the most of your recruiting efforts.

According to a recent poll done by SilkRoad, today's two top job search engines – Indeed and Simply Hired – account for the bulk of external online recruiting activity, namely 62% of interviews and 59% of hires...

SilkRoad, which offers cloud-based talent management solutions, also found Indeed delivered more than six times as many interviews as CareerBuilder, the next largest external source, and yielded nearly two and a half times as many hires as all the other top branded external sources combined (i.e. CareerBuilder, Craigslist, LinkedIn and Monster).

Employee referrals dominate recruiting among internal sources, producing 40% of interviews and 37% of hires, while ranking number one for hires among all the sources in the study.

Are you using any of these sites?

_____

Do you have an employee referral program to source top talent?

_____

If you don't have a referral program, do you think it's reasonable to add one?

_____

What tactics have performed well for you in recent years?

_____

_____

_____

Your network

For roles you're recruiting which are specific to your industry, you may want to consider an industry-specific job board, publication, or affiliated website. You could contact an industry accreditation organization to find out if you can post to their site or on their blog pages. If you have an accreditation through that organization you may even be able to post at a discount. Just ask!

Think about it. If you were looking for a job in your industry, where would you begin your search? If you have the same accreditation as your target candidates then you might logically gravitate to the same sources.

Your team members

Who knows your company's culture better than you? Who knows the type of skills that are needed on the team? Who knows the type of personalities that complement your existing team?

Your team members just might know more about your company than you do. Easier than training a recruiting firm about your industry or culture – and I'd argue it's money better spent – consider asking your current employees to help you find the best talent.

Your team members are not going to recruit people they won't want to work with. They aren't going to refer lazy people. And remember – you're going to interview and make the final decision of who joins the team. Employee referral programs can be a powerful piece of your recruiting strategy!

And it's cost effective. Most employee referral programs pay associates between $250 and $1,000 based on the success of the referred new hire. That's significantly less than a recruiting or temporary agency's fees. What's better is that you're investing in your future by investing in the input of your current team members. Money well spent!

Ask for team input

Don't be intimidated by this type of discussion. Your management team should add their thoughts to your recruiting strategy.

- What recruiting tools worked well for them at previous employers?
- What industry partners do they think would have great talent?
- How could you utilize their network of contacts to source great talent?

Your challenge

I challenge you to do two simple things *this week* to transform your hiring practices:

- Visit Indeed.com and look at your company profile. They already set one up for you. You've had no control over what's listed there so far, but all the candidates for your positions are reading this listing. Enhance your company profile and make sure there are clear ways for candidates to find your openings when they want to submit their resumes.

- Implement an employee referral program to reward your current staff for submitting top talent. No one knows your company culture and practices better than your existing team. Wouldn't you rather give a bonus to a valued employee for finding a new team member than to a stranger at a recruiting agency? You know your budget better than I do, but if you're willing to pay 20-30% placement fee to an agency, I bet you can afford a $500 referral bonus to your employees.

The point of recruiting is to find the most qualified candidates for your company's jobs. The analogies are endless, but you can't fish in the same pond for different kinds of talent. Diversify your practices just as you do with your sales and marketing strategies.

Attracting Your Team

Company growth is the goal of most business owners. It's a sign of success and a reward for your hard work. It also comes with complications, one of which is determining who will join your team to help you continue such prosperous growth. Let's start with recruitment!

Attracting candidates to your business is an industry in and of itself. There is a great deal of psychology that goes along with candidate attraction. Think about it – what attracted you to the business you lead? How did you decide to work in your industry? Answering some of those questions can help lead you to the best way to attract candidates who have related interests to your company.

As a reminder, candidates will use the posted job description to determine not only if their experiences are a good fit for you, but also *if your needs are a good fit for them.*

Read that again!

Candidate attraction is a little bit about the job and *a lot* about how someone will fit into your company. Employee engagement strategies suggest that people focus on "What's in it for me?" as the first and foremost part of their decision-making process.

This is true, even at the initial recruitment stage. In addition to listing work that needs to be performed and required experiences and skills, your job posting should also include information about your company, an indication of your culture, what benefits the position offers, and anything else you can think of that would make an employee want to choose your business as the next step in their career path.

How can you target the right candidates?

Have you ever thought that we live in a world where the Internet rules? Well, it's true. And because of that, the way you will find top talent, and the way top talent will find you, is through the algorithms written by people we don't know and will never know. These same people know nothing about your business. They simply write the code that connects you with the right talent for your team.

You have control over this – believe it or not! Here's an example. If you're traveling out of town and have a craving for pizza... but you don't want to go to just any place... what's the first thing you do? You probably pull out your trusty phone and type into a browser: *"Where's the best pizza place?"*

That browser takes your request and compares it to all the websites that have "best pizza place" in their site or reviews. You just did a keyword search.

Your control in targeting the best candidates in the internet sea is via keywords. Use these keywords in your job posting to lead the right candidates to find your openings.

When you include the features of your company and the job opening through the right keywords, you will appeal to the candidates who best fit your needs. It's the fastest way for you to draw in the targeted candidates who are the best fit for your team. Companies who find the best talent use these tactics. You should be doing this, too!

Let's look at this sample posting from the last section from Top Notch Technologies. It's loaded with keywords!

> Top Notch Technologies has an opportunity for an Accountant to join its Houston, TX location. Our success is based on our employees working as a team in every aspect of the business. Our finance team supports each of our company's profit centers by working closely with other department leaders like sales, operations, IT, and customer support. Each person is a partner and a team member – whether it's working on projects, special assignments or your very important "day job"!

Your career

A successful accounting career at Top Notch Technologies will have the opportunity to partner with other departments through project participation and project management. The career path for this team includes taking on successively challenging roles on the finance team as well as cross-functional project teams and opportunities to transfer to other departments to broaden your skills.

The opportunity

To be successful in the current opening as an accountant requires someone who is a great communicator, team player, someone who feels confident voicing his/her opinion on the right decisions for the business and someone who has the following experiences:

Monthly account reconciliation

Using an ERP or similar accounting system on a daily basis

Creating reports and performing analysis on the data

Posting entries and making necessary corrections to the general ledger (GL)

Proficient knowledge in the Microsoft Suite like Excel, Word, PowerPoint and Outlook

Bachelor's Degree (BA or BS) in accounting, finance, or general business from an accredited 4-year institution

Minimum of 4 years experience with general accounting practices

Prefer someone who has achieved the CPA accreditation or who has started the process toward achieving the CPA

When candidates search for job openings, they will load these keywords into the search feature of an Internet browser or a job board. If you're doing an online posting, this is the key to your success!

Networking – the Old New-fashioned Way

"What's old is new again."

That's right! The old-fashioned way of networking to find the best talent is once again in fashion. These tried and tested methods of searching through college alumni networks, trade associations, and similar methods are *en vogue* like never before.

Even though the method to attract people in those talent pools has changed (i.e. online job boards instead of printed magazines), you can still use some of the methods you always used. For example, you can email your job postings to your network. Be sure to include your fellow alums – and as an added bonus it's a good way to stay in touch with former colleagues and college friends.

For industry and trade associations, you can post information on their sites for a fee. Use the keyword method we talked about in the previous section. Make sure the physical location of the position is clearly stated and whether you will offer relocation assistance.

Job boards are not a new phenomenon but they're gaining new life. The job boards – particularly Indeed and CareerBuilder – have started to transform their approach to being a service to the candidate *and* the employer. These are very different approaches, so read on to make sure you use each effectively.

Indeed is the largest search engine geared to career search in the world, as of this book's publication. I refer to Indeed.com as a search engine because that's their method. They do not describe their site as a job board, so while there is a job board element, it's geared mainly to candidates researching companies, posting their opinions of employers, and... yes, searching for jobs.

Indeed.com "scrapes" other job boards and company websites. That's right. They do all the work for you – just like a search engine. But also like a search engine, your jobs have to be populated with the right keywords so the SEO works correctly! Indeed's efforts to scrape the Internet for job postings is why it's the largest job board on the planet.

A few things to be wary of:

Indeed.com is your friend. But it can be your foe. If you are an employer who doesn't treat team members very well, chances are Indeed is a place where your disgruntled employees will write a review. Similar to a site called GlassDoor, these reviews cannot be removed. And it takes a lot for the reviews to be edited. It doesn't matter if the posts are true, or grossly exaggerated. You can't remove them.

Another thing to be wary of is that you can't control the posting's content or the method for people to apply for a job unless you pay to promote your posting on Indeed. Why is that important? Well, if you update a posting – adjust a job title, or make other changes – they will likely not appear on Indeed. You will either need to get the posting right the first time, post a whole new listing, or pay to promote a job opening on Indeed.

You also cannot remove job postings from Indeed unless you've paid for the posting to be promoted by the company, meaning you paid for your posting to appear in the top five returns for certain keywords. (Yes, this is beginning to sound like Google.) Otherwise, you may end up receiving resumes for jobs that closed long ago or you may receive sales calls from recruiting agencies after you fill a position in another way.

CareerBuilder is one of the oldest job boards around. It started around the same time as Monster.com and has always played "second fiddle" to other boards. You can, however, have major impact by partnering with CareerBuilder, which positions itself as a full scale marketing partner for your business.

You will not always have open jobs at your company, but when you do, you want to fill them quickly with the best candidates possible. I don't have to tell you that's a tough order to fill if you start at ground zero, right? CareerBuilder knows that too, so it's developed a way to help you convert cold traffic to warm traffic with the use of content marketing tactics. You can then search your pool of "warm" candidates when you have a job opening that meets their skill sets.

Another tool for your talent acquisition strategy is LinkedIn. LinkedIn has been referred to as the modern day Chamber of Commerce. It's that and so much more. You may be using LinkedIn as a way to find targeted customers for your business. (HINT: if you're not using LinkedIn for this – start doing it now!) You can also use LinkedIn as a way to find top talent and network to discover people who are already knowledgeable about your industry.

What started as a business networking site has evolved into one of the hottest recruiting sources since the first job board back in the mid-1990s. LinkedIn is a generalist source for candidates as much as it is an industry-focused source. You can search for candidates based on skills, experience, or current/past employers. You can even find out who's currently working for your competitors. WOW! Where else can you find that kind of detail? Almost nowhere.

I'm a huge fan of LinkedIn, and as someone who has spent her entire career handling recruitment I can say LinkedIn has revolutionized the way the process works. (No offense to Monster.com which is the first innovator of the online job board.) LinkedIn allows you to see candidate information and the prospective employees can see *you* and your company.

That has created a big difference in the conversation now. Candidates can become very well educated on *you*. Be prepared. Your profile needs to be up-to-date if you're reaching out to candidates via LinkedIn. Candidates will tend to research both you and your company. They will also probably ask you questions during the pre-screening and interview process.

ACTION - For a guide to learn all there is to know about building your company brand on LinkedIn, visit:

www.business.linkedin.com/talent-solutions/company-career-pages?u=0#

Think about "the gig economy"

Hiring people isn't for every business and it's not for every leader. I can speak from experience that selecting the right people to join your team isn't a science and it has given me more than a little anxiety over the years. You can probably empathize. One way you can scale your business without hiring people, though, is through the growing and thriving gig economy.

It used to be that if you needed to fill a temporary spot within your business you'd contact a staffing firm and hire someone through their agency. That's still a great option for you and perhaps you even use those services now. If you are using agencies to source talent, then you also know it's quite costly. Sometimes it's too costly for small businesses and instead of a financial expense to the business, an owner might choose to give more assignments to existing staff. However, the cost of overworking team members shouldn't go unnoticed even though it won't show on your P&L.

The current gig economy is one that helps entrepreneurs and large businesses alike. Gone are the days when you had to struggle to find a talented, capable, and experienced professional in your area of need. Sites like Fiverr.com and Upwork.com connect you with graphic designers, personal assistants, engineers – name your need, name your price, and name your timeline... and you'll have your project completed without the burden of hiring a new team member. Wow!

These sites have helped me immensely. If I need a graphic created overnight I have my tried-and-true designer in Singapore whip something up while I sleep. When I wake up on East Coast time in the U.S., the work is there for me. Wonderful!

A word of caution regarding the hiring of contractors and consultants, though. I wouldn't be a strong HR partner to you if I didn't help educate you on the differences between true contractors and employees. This is an area where businesses of all sizes get into trouble, most famously Microsoft which paid $97M to end a temp-worker lawsuit.

Generally if you're controlling how things are done, supplying the tools for people to perform their work, and managing their performance, you may be in an employment relationship rather than a contractor relationship.

Here's a guide to help you, but keep in mind that if you fear you're verging on violation of this thing called "co-employment," contact your attorney for a thorough review:

- Do you require your contractors to sign employment documents like an I-9, W-4, etc., but do not pay them through your standard payroll system?
- Do you tell your contractors they must work for your company and only your company for more than 6 months?
- Have you asked your contractors to sign a non-competition agreement and tried to enforce the agreement?
- Do you supply your contractors with a laptop, mobile phone, company car, or similar devices?

If you answered yes to one or more of these questions you may be at risk for violating the IRS's definition of co-employment or common law employment.

To learn more, check out this great article from the American Marketing Association:

www.ama.org/career/Pages/Co-Employment-Liability-What-Every-Brand-and-Agency-Needs-to-Know.aspx

Interviewing

Who is going to help you fulfill your mission? Who is going to help your business scale to the size and scope you're targeting?

Other people.

That's right – you cannot do this alone.

Whether you take the route of hiring a contractor, consultant, or a direct employee, you have to create your ideal candidate profile and interview applicants before selecting them.

I can't express enough how important it is to plan ahead. It's to your benefit but it's also to the benefit of the candidate. If you've gotten this far to have a slate of candidates you want to get to know, now isn't the time to fly by the seat of your pants. This is your chance to make an impression in person. And this is often where I've seen employers fail. Tell me if this sounds familiar to you:

> Susan Eames is scheduled for an interview at 8:30 A.M. and she arrives early at 8:15. The boss is tied up in a meeting until 8:45 but sends his apologies to the receptionist via text who passes those regards onto Susan who's patiently waiting in the lobby.
>
> The boss rushes to the lobby as soon as he can, around 8:50. He escorts Susan to the conference room until he realizes he forgot to reserve the space and it's taken by someone else's meeting. Plan B – he decides to interview Susan in his office and now the time is 9 A.M.
>
> He hurriedly reviews Susan's background on her resume because he didn't have time to review it earlier. He starts scribbling bits and pieces of her responses to his questions but really all he's thinking about is who's slated to meet with Susan next and whether he's completely screwed up the interview schedule because his 8 A.M. meeting ran late ... By the time he wraps up with Susan and escorts her to

the next interview team member, it's 9:35, and he's late for another meeting.

When 5:30 P.M. rolls around on Susan's interview day he finally gets a chance to review his notes but can't make heads or tails of it because he didn't take the time to write thorough ideas of her experiences and skills.

Now what?

The scenario with Susan can be salvaged! The boss could talk to other interview team members about their perspective on Susan. He could schedule Susan for a second-round interview. He could check Susan's professional references.

But wouldn't it have been better to get all of the details from Susan in the first interview?

Yes. It would have been better for both the boss and Susan!

Preparation prior to the interview is key. Spend time beforehand and the interview will be a much more rewarding experience for you and the candidate.

How do you get to know a candidate?

Well, think about it this way – how do you get to know anyone? Start by asking questions. Unlike the pickup lines at your local watering hole (Hey baby, what's your sign?), you want to think through your questions ahead of time to make sure they warrant the right answers. Preparing questions that are targeted on background, experience, and skills of your candidates is essential to a successful interview. It will also keep you out of the pitfalls of interviewing – like asking questions that verge on being inappropriate or subject to federally protected classes.

How do you know what questions to ask?

Use your position description as your guide. You already thought about the type of work that needs to be accomplished by this role and what types of minimum experience and skills the candidate should possess to be successful.

Try this – if the job requires the person to perform account reconciliation on a daily basis, then ask a question that would target the candidates' experience like: "Describe for me the process you've used to reconcile accounts at your current company." Seems simple, right? It really is!

Stick with questions that are targeted to the person's real experience, real education, and real knowledge. Avoid asking questions that target hypothetical answers like: "Susan, if you needed to perform account reconciliation on a daily basis, how would you set up your spreadsheet?" Instead, ask Susan for a specific example: "At your last company, walk me through the process of performing account reconciliation. Include the systems or software you used and other people you connected with to provide/receive data."

See the difference? You want to know what Susan has actually done in the past versus how she *might* do something in the future.

For a list of 103 interview questions and other interviewing tips and tools visit OperamHR.com/book
Click on the HIRE section and enter code: SimpleHR
Look for 103 Interview Questions

How do you avoid getting into hot water?

I feel like the leaders I've supported over my career are in one of two camps on this topic. Either they are oblivious to the laws or they are paralyzed by not knowing the laws. Either way it's not a good start to getting to know a candidate during the interview.

Simple rule: Stay away from personal data that might not directly determine someone's race, religion, or gender that is protected but still gets to the point. For example, if you want to know if a candidate has children – don't ask if they have children. The question and answer are likely not relevant to the person being able to perform the job duties. But what matters is whether they are able to report to work on the necessary days and times. So instead, ask a question like: "Are there any foreseeable reasons you would have a problem arriving on time at 8 A.M. and leaving at 5 P.M. Monday through Friday?"

What about note taking? Can I take notes or will that get me in trouble?

Good question! Just like what questions you ask, you should be mindful about what you record from the conversation. First of all, don't record it on camera or recording device as that breaches a number of privacy laws. If you take handwritten or typed notes as someone is speaking, be sure your notes are pertinent to the job qualifications – do not make notes on personal appearance, gender, disability, race, or religion. If someone comes across as having difficulty articulating thoughts, then write "difficulty articulating thoughts" rather than "gives stupid answers."

Remember to write notes that you will understand later, otherwise you'll be back at your desk at the end of the day and have no idea what the candidate told you at the 8:30 A.M. interview!

Include cultural questions in your interview process

Earlier in the book I gave you tips on writing position descriptions, posting your job, and tips on how to convey the culture of the company. Now we are at the stage of interviewing candidates. You definitely want to select a candidate based on skills and abilities. But what about cultural fit? If you thought selecting a candidate based on skills and abilities was tough (all somewhat objective criteria), making a selection about cultural fit (subjective criteria) is a whole other ball game.

In addition to asking questions about work-related experiences and confirming education, you should consider peppering the interview with questions focused on preferences:

- What is important to you in a work place?
- What types of work do you like to perform?
- Do you enjoy working in a group or independently?

These types of questions are indicators of what is important to the prospective employee. It allows you to decipher if you have a match between what's important to them and what's important to you. By using these types of questions intermingled with objective, skill-based questions you're also engaging candidates by considering what's important to them.

Give a tour

You work at your company every day. You know where the kitchen is located. And you know how many steps it takes to get to the nearest bathroom. There's also a section of cubicles at the end of the hall... But guess what? Your candidate doesn't know any of those things.

Your candidate is about to make a decision to either stay where they are or work for you. Believe it or not, things like the condition of the kitchen, the bathrooms, and who works at your company are pretty big influencers on a decision to accept your offer.

People spend more time at work than they do anywhere else during the waking day. Show them the work environment. Don't be embarrassed about the chipped flooring in the kitchen or the color of the paint on the walls. This is your business, warts and all! Candidates need to understand the working environment as they make their decision.

Go with your gut

You've probably heard that advice before. Maybe you've even used that advice before. I am not telling you that you shouldn't follow your instincts. You're a successful business person and on more than one occasion I am certain you've relied on your instinct to get you through a tough situation. And I hope that's worked out for you!

Determining whether a candidate is a good cultural fit for your company definitely takes into account your opinions and impressions. But don't use your gut as your sole decision making factor. Consider the candidates' words and feedback from the interview process and how what's important to them aligns with what's important to you.

Want more brass tacks of interviewing?

Over the course of time, some of my blog readers have asked about what to do during the interview itself. I wanted to dedicate this section to helping you navigate through the interview.

Many interviews I've been through as a candidate have had a similar format: Ask me to summarize my resume; Ask me to give examples about my work history; Ask me crazy off the wall questions to try to trip me up. Rarely do they ask me what questions I have. Rarely do they plan a facility tour (because "we'll do that at the second interview.") Rarely do they follow up after the interview.

You're not going to be like those companies anymore!

Resume

Ask questions about the resume. You want to make sure the candidate has been truthful in what's listed on the resume and that you understand the chronology of experience and skills. Does the resume match the online profile, like LinkedIn? Which one lists more details? Don't hesitate to ask questions about those discrepancies!

Some other questions that will give you good perspective on the candidate's mindset and goals can be asked during the resume phase of your interview. Here are some samples:

- Why did you change jobs?
- What did you gain by changing jobs?
- Do you have any regrets about positions you changed? If so, why?
- Skill set – Confirm the skills listed on the resume or online profiles. If the candidate includes programming and coding skills, ask questions using a common vocabulary that anyone with a degree of knowledge will understand. Then press the next questions with successively more detailed level of vocabulary or complexity of issues. That will test the candidate's knowledge.
- Training – If the candidate lists leading a significant project on the LinkedIn profile, but does not have a PMP certification, ask questions about that. Confirm the candidate indeed *led* the project and didn't just *participate*. Confirm that the candidate does or does not want a PMP certification and why.

Experiences

A candidate's past experiences are going to be the strongest indicator of success in the future. Whatever the candidate has learned in school or on the job, whatever projects have been assigned, or whatever goals have been failed or achieved are going to be examples of what will be brought to your company. Now is the time to ask as many questions as you can about that training or work experience.

The way you phrase the questions will help or hinder a thorough response. I've recommended to clients that they take one project and hammer away at the questions. Here's a sample:

Q1: Susan, we want to get to know your background as thoroughly as we can. Can you think of one project or task during your past that we could use to get to know you better?

Q2: What is that task/project and at which company did you have this experience?

Q3: Describe the task/project for me. Give as many details as you can to help give me perspective.

Q4: How did this task/project impact the business?

Q5: What was your role in this task/project?

Q6: Who did you work with to accomplish this task/project?

Q7: How did you interact with others with this task/project? Mainly via email, phone, lots of meetings, etc.?

Q8: What went well with the task/project?

Q9: What didn't go well with this task/project?

Q10: Did you offer any ideas for process improvements or bring forth other ideas to challenge the standard processes?

Q10a: If so, what were those ideas?

Q10b: Were any of those ideas adopted? Tell me what was selected and why.

Within these ten questions you will get to know Susan's experiences at a whole different level than asking only: "Tell me about a project you worked on."

Behaviors

If the top frustrations are about behaviors, then shouldn't you ask those questions in the interview?

The resume, LinkedIn profile, Facebook timeline, and Twitter feed will give you insights into your candidate. You can spend an entire interview with someone asking about what you've read in print or online about them. But I will argue with you that you get only a partial picture of someone if you spend your time on just those things. The top frustration my clients have with employees is about behaviors – employees with good behaviors they want to replicate, or employees with bad behaviors they want to terminate!

If you need someone with great customer service skills, how can you get to know that in the interview? The key is through asking what are often referred to as behavioral interview questions. These questions target past actions in the candidate's work history as an indicator of how a candidate will act while employed by you. You build these questions to solicit open-ended answers, not just a yes or no.

As a bonus to you, I've prepared over 100 behavioral interview questions, separated for you by behavior type.

- Team work
- Communication
- Quality of work
- Customer Focus
- Prioritizing
- Process improvement
- Dependability
- Integrity

Leading a Team

- Change Management
- Strategic Thinking
- Planning and Organizing
- Understanding Business Operations

Visit: OperamHR.com/book
Click on the HIRE section and enter code: SimpleHR
Look for 103 Interview Questions

Use an interview team

At the beginning of this section I reminded you that you can't scale and expand your business alone. You will need help. I'd argue the same point about making decisions on hiring team members. You can't get to the bottom of all this alone. But you can divide and conquer.

There are multiple ways I've suggested to get to know a candidate better during the interview. If you have a group of people on the interview team, you can assign each of these (resume, skill set, experience, and behaviors) to an interview team member. Voila! You will have an interview plan.

Interviewing is your chance to learn as much about candidates as absolutely possible. Candidates are multi-dimensional. Make sure your interview digs into more than just one dimension of someone's background.

Evaluating candidates

The greatest challenge you'll have is to objectively decide which candidate meets your needs and fits your culture. It is sometimes easier to make the decision subjectively, i.e. Go with Your Gut! But an objective path is the better practice. Why? Well, beyond the equal employment compliance that your business is obligated to uphold, it may also be easier to decide based on the facts rather than the fiction.

We've laid out a process that builds on itself. Let me give you a refresher:

- ☐ When you created the job posting, you decided on the required experiences, skills, education, and behaviors that are necessary for the job.
- ☐ You posted that job to targeted talent.
- ☐ You received resumes of qualified candidates.
- ☐ You evaluated those candidates or screened them based on the criteria in the job posting.
- ☐ You created an interview team. You assigned the interview team questions based on the experiences, skills, education, and behaviors essential for the job.

Now you're going to evaluate the interviewed candidates based on their responses to those questions and their alignment with the job's needs. Further, the candidates are going to differentiate themselves by the level of experience or skills above and beyond their competition.

I have evaluation forms for you on the website based on each behavioral competency – and I included sample interview questions that will target specific behavior. Check them out online. I think you'll find them to be very helpful. But here's a sample:

Candidate Evaluation Guide

Instructions
- ☐ Use interview questions to target certain behaviors related to the position you're recruiting to fill.
- ☐ Assign no more than 3 behaviors to each interview team member to target as part of their evaluation of the candidates.
- ☐ Use each interview team member's evaluation as part of the selection process.

Rating Scale

Candidate Rating Scale		
0	No response	Candidate did not answer the question.
1	Basic knowledge	Candidate's response shows evidence of basic use of behavior.
2	Moderate knowledge	Candidate's response shows proficiency with the behavior.
3	Considerable knowledge	Candidate's response shows high level of proficiency with behavior.

Evaluation

Team Work	0	1	2	3
Candidate considers the viewpoints of others; respects others	☐	☐	☐	☐
Willingness to assist others	☐	☐	☐	☐
Puts success of team above own interests	☐	☐	☐	☐
Skills Assessment				
Candidate's education matches requirements of job	☐	☐	☐	☐
Candidate uses required skills to the level needed to be successful in this job.	☐	☐	☐	☐

For a detailed description of the Candidate Evaluation Guide as well as samples of each behavior, visit OperamHR.com/book
Click on the HIRE section and enter code: SimpleHR
Look for Candidate Evaluation Worksheet

Why Marketing is HR's New BFF

Imagine that you're a new employee. You saw a company's awesome website and online content as you researched the position you were planning to win. And now you're there. You landed your dream job. Wow – so exciting!

But when you go to the orientation... well... there's no consistency. The policies feature one logo and the benefits brochures have another. The policies are dated from the mid-2000s, and you're not even sure you joined the same company you interviewed with. What's the deal?

The deal is probably that the HR team is so swamped with getting the right benefits program set up for you, scheduling your orientation, getting your manager to prepare on-boarding training for you, and setting up your new office that it never dawned on them that establishing an HR brand was important.

Is your company's marketing focused on outward branding and messaging, but perhaps you haven't thought about the power of internal branding?

I'd like to challenge you to think about your business as a brand and your employees as consumers of that company brand. In a way, your employees are your most important client. When you don't have a strong team supporting your business, things become very difficult for you as a leader. Putting forth the effort to attract a team is only part of your puzzle. Showing that you are committed to them joining and staying on your team is the solution.

Think about your internal brand as the way you're going to do business with your employees. Just like your company's external brand includes font type and size, colors, and images, your internal brand guide should include things like:

- The tone you'll use in your internal communications
- Policies, handbook, email, company meetings, etc.
- The flexibility of your workforce
- Dress code, core working hours, work from home options, etc.
- The number of times employees will hear from leadership
- Monthly email blasts, quarterly all-hands meetings, video
- The level of transparency employees should expect related to compensation, performance, opportunity for advancement

When you develop a consistent approach to these things, your employees will identify with your company in a much closer manner – just like the customers and consumers of a product feel a connection with certain brands.

Take a deep breath about the level of work that might be involved with this. I am not suggesting you overhaul everything overnight... otherwise you risk losing the engagement of your team. On the contrary, take this one step at a time.

Here's a checklist that might be helpful for you:

- Does your recruiting page reflect the same brand imagery as the rest of your business?
- Do you communicate clearly the company's work/products, industry, and goals on the recruiting page?
- Do newly hired employees receive a welcome packet/email/website that shows the same brand imagery as the rest of your business?
- Do newly hired employees receive an introduction to the business when they start their employment?

- Have you created a video for your new hires that welcomes them to the company and communicates your general goals for the business?
- Does your management team understand the value of having periodic check-ins with their staff?

If you're feeling overwhelmed, take one thing from this list and implement it this quarter. Then take another task from this list and implement it six months later. One day at a time. One step at a time. Your candidates and employees *will* take notice.

Get Your House in Order

One last bit of preparation advice before we get into the details of bringing people onto your team. I want to make sure you're really ready to bring someone new into your organization. Whether you are hiring new staff – in office, eight-to-five, Monday through Friday – or bringing on a contractor or online freelancer, you want to make sure you're ready to incorporate these individuals into your team, so you don't end up sabotaging the entire thing because you're not ready.

Think of this process a bit like when you're preparing to have a baby. First, you have to think about all the things that go on in your house that you never thought about before. You need to install the little hooks on the kitchen cabinet doors. You have to put plugs in the electrical sockets, and padding around the coffee table, and a baby gate at the top of the stairs.

I'm not implying that employees are like your children, but you should be looking out for their best interests – because you're expecting them to look out for *your* best interests.

Get prepared. Think about it ahead of time. If you already have current employees, ask them if you made a good first impression. Show them the checklist at the end of this chapter. Probably they will say, "Yeah. If you had done that, it would have made my introduction to your business a lot better. I could have gotten to work for you a lot quicker."

What do I mean? I mean new employees will expect certain comforts and tools when they join your business. The following listing is not meant to scare you, but rather to prepare you so you don't find yourself in a tough spot.

Now, imagine if you were going to take a job, what are some of the things you would expect?

You would want a place to sit down. So there's a desk, a chair, some pens and maybe some paper, a printer, and maybe even a copier.

I know we live in an electronic age, but heaven knows we still have to file paper and physically mail some things. Make sure you're prepared for those eventualities.

Oh and while we're at it – since this is the electronic age – a laptop, mobile phone, Skype account, ERP account, email, etc., are essential, so get them set up before the candidate arrives. This may sound like detailed minutiae, but I have to tell you, even the largest corporations forget about what a new employee expects to see on their first day. While you no doubt expect the new hire to get started right away and get to work, if they don't have a computer, an email address, or a phone – and there's no plan to get any of those things set up – they will not feel welcomed, will not be able to get to work for you immediately, and may even wonder, "Why did I just quit my other job to come work here? What was I thinking?

Well, really. What were *they* thinking? And what were you thinking?

I know what you were thinking. You were thinking about a thousand other things: your customers, the finances of your business, and the next product or service you're coming out with.

This little bit of on-boarding minutiae needs to be part of your master hiring plan. We definitely don't want your new employee to be disappointed. You've made all the right impressions during the sourcing of candidates, during the interviews, and with all of your follow-up. The impression on the first day is either really hard to beat or is really tough to overcome during the new employee's tenure. You decide which side of the coin you'd like to be on.

Also make sure there's a fresh and tidy bathroom for someone working in your office space, and possibly a refrigerator and microwave for use at meal breaks. (And make sure you show them where those things are located!)

At the end of this chapter, you'll see a checklist of work space items to consider, but before you even get into those details, I want to talk a bit about the economics of your business – *before* you make a hiring decision.

Your CPA or third-party billing company is going to be a good partner as you decide who you can bring into your organization, and what can you afford to pay them. That CPA might say to you, "Look. You can't afford somebody forty hours a week. You can afford twenty-three hours a week at the most, and you can pay them $10 an hour."

If this is what your CPA is telling you, you should think long and hard about bringing an employee into your business (versus a contractor or freelancer). First, there are not a lot of part-time workers in the marketplace right now, so the numbers of potential great talent are fewer. I'm not saying those workers are not qualified. I'm simply saying the pool of people who are willing to work part-time hours is smaller. If you can only afford to hire someone part-time, you're not going to get a wide choice of candidates. You need to know that going into this venture.

Second, if you can only afford someone at $10 an hour, you need to make sure to do a bit of market research. Go online and check job boards to learn what the going rate is for the type of position you want to hire. From an affordability standpoint, ask yourself if that going rate makes sense for your finances, because if it doesn't, then you should probably go the contractor or freelance route.

If you've decided you are done investing your time into administrative tasks at your business, and you want to bring someone on who's going to make you even more effective and efficient by relieving you from those administrative tasks, then think about virtual assistants instead. Think about contracted individuals who can help reduce your administrative workload.

You may not actually need support for forty hours a week. Maybe you don't need to hire someone full-time after all. There are lots of great online resources where you can hire a freelancer or virtual assistant – somebody who you will never even see, but who will provide great work for you. Organizations like Upwork.com, Fiverr.com, and HireMyMom.com, can help you find talented people who don't want to work full-time, who don't necessarily need to work in an office space that requires you to put in a desk and a chair and a printer and a microwave (and to make sure you've cleaned the bathroom), but who can provide really great work for you.

Know your numbers first. Know what tasks you really need to get done, and make sure you're prepared to bring someone on board.

Finally, talk to your CPA or business attorney about what type of employment relationship you are going to create with your new hire, what sort of reporting is required, and what kind of documentation you should have. A Human Resources professional like me can help make sure you have all the documentation put in place. Your CPA or business attorney can help you decide how best to protect yourself – and not sabotage your business.

If you need a non-disclosure agreement or a confidentiality agreement so your intellectual property of products or services are protected, then by all means, add that into your employment process. Get those forms ready *before* you bring someone on staff.

For a more detailed worksheet on orientation and on-boarding, visit OperamHR.com/book

Click on the HIRE section and enter code: SimpleHR

Look for:
Orientation – Personnel File Checklist
Orientation – Hiring Manager Checklist
On-Boarding – First 60 Day

ENGAGE

Retaining Talent

What makes you a good boss?

There's this phrase, "The good boss." What does that mean, anyway?

It's a subjective term and rarely one you award to yourself. It's usually bestowed on a person by someone else. Whether it's "good boss" or "bad boss" (and we've seen the movie *Terrible Bosses*), I think we can agree we don't want to be one of the bad bosses.

What makes an employee bestow the title "good boss"?

It's tough to determine what makes a "good boss," and every person and organization has a different definition. I believe that much of it comes back to the nature of the people inside the organization and what *they* define as being a good boss. You can be a great manager of people in one organization yet be perceived as absolutely terrible in another.

Determining what your organization's culture is and building around it is going to be the key to your success. Here's an example for you:

> You determine that the company you work for – or the company you own – has a strong team culture. The organization values people working together, being collaborative, willing to respond to customers at the drop of a hat, and to be interactive with people both inside and outside the organization.
>
> Despite the organization's mindset, you start hiring a bunch of people who prefer to work solo, who resist team meetings, and abhor your continual push to collaborate.

Guess what? You are going to get the title of a bad boss. It's not necessarily going to be because of anything you're expecting. Your approach doesn't align with the business! You selected employees who are being asked to do work they are not naturally comfortable doing. It's going to take a lot of extra effort on the employees' part to be interactive and social and collaborative with others both inside and outside of the organization. Typically that doesn't work for anyone involved.

You need to set the tone and assemble a group of employees who are also aligned with the company's culture. And you should feel confident in making hiring or termination decisions with team members who will not fit in with the culture.

Read that again.

You should feel confident in making hiring or termination decisions with team members who will not fit in with the culture.

Assembling people who align with the culture of the organization has a higher likelihood for success. It also means you have a higher likelihood of success in leading the group and accomplishing goals.

Set up your team for success by clearly communicating the culture of the company in your job postings, talking about it openly during the interview process, selecting candidates who give examples of previous success in similar working environments, and managing the team's performance based on those expectations.

Also remember, in the example above, it's not the employees' fault if they don't align with your culture. They are not *wrong* for being introverted, and they are not *wrong* for being extroverted. What *is* wrong is hiring the opposite type of individual for the position and culture of the business.

If your business sells products and services through collaborative, with engaging customer service, and you hire individuals who absolutely hate answering the phone, you're going to have a big problem. And you will be considered the worst boss by holding them accountable for behaviors and traits they can't naturally fulfill.

Beyond the organization's culture, you need to determine your own personal strengths and weaknesses and assemble your job profile (and ultimately, your team) being mindful of the culture you want to cultivate in your organization. If you are a very extroverted person and you hire a lot of introverted individuals (because they're doing data analysis or they are software developers or they're working on intense engineering projects) they will want to work alone. They will desire a quiet space, and you could become the bull in the china shop, barging into their office on a regular basis.

That might not be the best mix. If you can tolerate, however, being a bit quieter, adjusting your natural personality to make sure those individuals are successful, then that's going to be a situation that works for you and your team.

A few take-away ideas from this section:

When you're preparing to hire new team members or prepping performance reviews, ask these questions:

- ☐ Why are you going to bring people into your organization?
  - Because you want to scale your business?
  - Because you need to assemble a group of people with a complementary set of skills to yours?
  - Because you need team members who can support your customers in a way you can't?
- ☐ How has your team responded to the needs of the organization?
- ☐ Was your team set up for success to meet the business's demands?
- ☐ What could you have done differently to help support your team members?

Remember, you're going to be a good boss if you:

- assemble team members who fulfill the skills you don't possess
- assemble team members who are complementary to each other
- assemble team members who are complementary to the type of work in your business

Your business may require different kinds of personalities to get the job done. Think about whether you need to target individuals who like working independently, or as part of a team. Those groups can coexist in an organization – with the right office environment, or work-from-home combination. But please don't confuse the two and ultimately get pegged as a bad boss.

Engagement

Engagement is not about being happy or unhappy. Engagement is about looking at the whole employee and tying their wants, their work, company goals, and recognition together. I learned these concepts from an engagement guru and New York Times best-selling author Kevin Kruse, who helped me understand that happiness is different from engagement. That was an important shift for me to make when I created engagement programs for my corporate employers.

Happiness is an ideal we all strive for. But if happiness is your goal of the engagement strategy, what happens when people are unhappy?

Since happiness is not a constant state for most people, is it okay for someone to be unhappy at the company and still be considered engaged?

4 Rules of Engagement

Do these questions sound familiar to you?

- How do you motivate the unmotivated?
- Why do my employees bother coming to work everyday? I could get more done if I did things myself!
- What can I do to make my team more productive?

I've asked myself these questions a time or two during my management career. If you've managed team members at all – whether it was a direct management relationship or leadership during a project you managed – it's easy to think that sometimes those around you don't have as much motivation as you. When I am in that situation, I take a step back and ask myself, "Why is this happening?"

When my team doesn't seem motivated it's usually because they don't have the same vision as I do. Let me rephrase that. Often what's happened is that I created a plan but didn't share it clearly with my team. I can see what we need to do, why we are doing this, and what is the end result. But if my team seems unmotivated it's because I didn't clearly communicate and educate as often as needed.

Employee engagement has four pillars, as I see it. (Let's be clear that I didn't create these concepts!)

#1 - What's in it for me?

#2 - Do I understand the company's/project's goals?

#3 - Do I understand how I contribute to the success of those goals?

#4 - Do I feel rewarded and recognized for my contributions?

This is the easiest how-to guide you'll ever get for employee motivation. These four simple questions can be applied to every presentation, one-on-one meeting, team meeting, or goal setting discussion. If you use an approach that reflects how you've considered the employee's perspective and achievement of their personal goals you will be more successful.

Working harder, working more hours, providing more output – that's what the company wants.

Achieving goals, progressing in a career path, and receiving rewards and recognition are why an employee might want to put forth extra effort and deliver high results.

"Corporate trust" is a buzz-worthy phrase used in corporations around the world. Developing trust with clients is important to sustained revenue and development opportunities. Corporate responsibilities can also relate to environmental responsibilities and other external-facing needs for a corporation to be trusted.

Developing trust with employees is an inward-facing process. It's often not on the priority list for struggling companies to find broken areas of their culture. (Have you read *The Five Dysfunctions of a Team* by Patrick Lencioni? If not, do so immediately!) The trust of your workforce is important for multiple reasons but too often the mention of "our leaders will go to jail if YOU break the law" or "we must comply with XYZ laws" outweighs why corporate trust is important for employees.

Following the first principle of employee engagement – What's in it for me? – employees have to understand why they should trust the company, as much as how they should show that trust.

Engagement Point #1 – What's In It for Me?

What is the employment experience at your company?

Employees get to know you even before they're employees. It happens even before they are candidates. People might get to know your company as customers, visitors, or through your network. They get an impression of you even before employment is a topic. When you develop your sales and marketing strategies you think about messaging, consistency and targeting an audience. The talent pipeline works the same way both before and after employment begins.

Let's break it down into pieces:

- How do you find candidates to join your company?
- What is the first impression a candidate has about your company?
- What's the tone of manager-employee relations after employment begins?
- How often do employees hear about the financial or growth vision of the company?
- Have you promoted someone on your team in the last year?

These questions are for you to start thinking about the employee's view of the employment experience at your company. I like to call this the "employment life cycle" and sometimes I refer to it as the employee value proposition. It doesn't matter what you call it. It only matters if you're putting thought and action into it.

When you start thinking about the employment life cycle from the perspective of an employee rather than the employer, your culture will start to shift. What do I mean by that? Let's consider some scenarios.

Recruitment

If you've spent any time reading job postings you'll notice one thing pretty quickly – most companies copy and paste their internal job description directly into the online posting site and wait for the best talent to magically appear. If you read the first part of this book you know my thoughts on that. In case you're unsure, I don't think this is the best approach. Why? Because you're not presenting to the best talent why they should choose your company over others and how this job will fit into their career path.

If you are going to make a job change, it better be for a good reason, right? You spend more time at work than anywhere else. You spend more time thinking about work than anything else. You spend more money on education leading you to your job. And the list goes on and on. So if you're trying to hire the best talent for your company, shouldn't you try to appeal to those candidates by presenting what's in it for them to join your company?

The hiring process is about telling a story. You are presenting to candidates the story of your company and describing the opportunity so they can see themselves in the position. When you start presenting job opportunities from the perspective of the candidate rather than just the needs of the company, you'll see a drastic change in the quality of candidates who apply.

Don't get me wrong, you aren't going to completely eliminate the "lookey-loos" who will apply to any job regardless of their match in qualifications or experience. But you will appeal to a higher caliber of candidate by writing from their perspective. Here is an example:

Basic job posting:

> Top Notch is looking to hire an accountant. Only CPAs and BS in Accounting need apply. Must also have 5 years of accounting experience. Email your resume to jobs@topnotch.net

Job posting written with top talent in mind:

> Are you looking to take the next step in your accounting career but feel limited at your current company? Top Notch is seeking to hire someone just like you to fill a mid- to senior-level General Accountant position. Ideally we would like someone who has handled the monthly closing

process, can investigate and close out discrepancies in accounts, perform bank reconciliation, and can do higher level analysis to share with upper management on the financial performance of the company. If this sounds like an advancement in your career or you'd like to know more, email us your resume and questions at jobs@topnotch.net

Performance

Performance management programs have gotten complicated. Extremely complicated. So much so that I think managers and employees cringe at the thought of going through the dreaded annual review process. I don't blame you if you dislike performance management programs you've experienced during your career. I didn't think much of them either – and I often represented the department who authored these awful programs.

You know why they are sometimes awful? The programs are focused on data the company needs to extract and analyze rather than the crux of the process – which is to check in on and improve the performance of team members. In our pursuit to check on the health of the organization we've lost sight of what really matters.

Performance discussions that focus on what's in it for employees and their managers are simple and frequent. The more frequent the conversations the less complicated they are and truly less stressful. Think about it this way. If I (as the employee) have a monthly conversation with you about what I did in that period of time I am probably more likely to remember the course of events, the work I did to achieve my goals, and you (as the manager) will be able to applaud me or redirect my activities to be more in line with what you want. I am also able to see how my performance impacts my goals, my future, my income, and the way I fit into the organization.

This is much less stressful for both of us because the conversation can be 30-45 minutes instead of 60-90 minutes. These shorter, more frequent check-ins make the process much more aligned with what's in it for both the employee and the manager.

Succession Planning

You may not have a formal succession planning program at your company but if you promoted anyone in the organization recently you conducted a step in the succession process. And good for you if that happened at your organization!

When a candidate applies for a job they may be thinking about your company as an advancement in their career. So during their employment it's helpful to continue the conversations about how their work will help them advance. Advancement means different things to different people. If you have a small organization you might not be able to offer promotions to team members often. But you may not have to in order to keep team members engaged. Ask your employees what they view as advancement. It might mean working on more complicated projects or interacting with a higher level of customer or taking a third party training program. When you get to know what's in it for the employee you can better prepare and steer the succession of their work to support achieving your business's goals.

Engagement Point #2 - Do I understand the company's goals and objectives?

Tell them what you're thinking

"I can't read your mind."

Have you heard that before? Maybe it was from a significant other or your children. Maybe it was from members on a volleyball or basketball team you play on.

Wherever you've heard it before, the fact remains that no one but you knows the thoughts in your head. When you work with people day in and day out and don't say the thoughts that are in your head, you're a mystery. Worse than that, you might be the proverbial thorn in everyone's side.

I was talking with a client about a recent resignation from his team. He was upset and rightfully so. This employee worked for the company for 6 years. He was on a very successful track. The employee was involved in activities with the company. And this isn't a stodgy company. This company has a progressive approach for getting employees involved with complex client matters and project management. My client thought he was doing the right things to keep his team members engaged and employed with him for the long run.

The thing is that even when you do what you think are the right things, the employees might not know what you're thinking. Or they might have a very different perspective.

What's someone to do in this situation?

Communicate.

Talk with your team members about what's happening with the strategy for the company, a team you lead, or a project you're leading.

Solicit input from your team members on the direction a project needs to go. Act on those suggestions.

Give communications events strong weight in your company's culture – meaning don't say you're going to have these meetings and give up, cancel, or postpone them.

Have one-to-one meetings with your team members that are frequent and somewhat informal. The more you talk with each other about your questions, their questions, and everyone's game plans, the more effective your entire organization will be.

Get the thoughts out of your head and out into the open. Talk frequently and openly. Include your colleagues or subordinates in decision making. Hold each other accountable for getting the work done.

Engagement Point #3 – Do I understand how I contribute to the company's success?

It starts with orientation and on-boarding.

Imagine again that you're a new employee. You saw the company's awesome website and content online as you researched this company you were planning to join. And now you're here. You landed your dream job.

But at orientation, there are no consistent messages. The "last updated" date on the policies is from a different century, and the company logos on the handbook don't match. What's the deal?

As we mentioned in the Hire section, this scenario comes about when the HR team is consumed with other tasks: benefits programs, scheduling, setting up office and network equipment, and coordinating with supervisors and managers to get new staff on-boarded.

It never dawned on anyone in leadership that an HR brand was important to consider. After all, the right job descriptions were written. The position was posted on all the right job boards. And the most qualified candidates were interviewed.

Now that your new team member has been selected, what do you do next?

The terms "orientation" and "on-boarding" are sometimes used interchangeably but they are actually quite different.

"Orientation" is a program for your business to acquire information from your new employee and give a general introduction. "On-boarding" is a longer introduction to your new team member to the company, colleagues, and performance requirements.

Do you remember your first day with your current employer?

Orientation

Orientation typically happens on the first day of a new team member's time with your company. Did you sit in a room with an HR Representative going through a stack of papers? Did you fully read every policy document before you signed it? Doubtful. There probably wasn't time to get through everything in detail.

Some companies start orientation before the first day to try to give newly hired team members a chance to review documents, read and understand policies, and prepare questions ahead of their first day. This is a great idea and a best practice for orientation. You can load your employment documents on a secure site (or an extranet to your intranet page), you could bundle your orientation documents into an Adobe PDF Portfolio document, or at the very least mail the hard copy documents to the new team member as far in advance as possible. Be sure you clearly mark which documents are for review and which documents need to be signed or initialed by the new team member.

On-boarding

On-boarding usually follows the Day 1 orientation session, but can be introduced to new team members before their start date. While orientation is usually an HR-driven event, on-boarding is a collaborative effort between the hiring manager, department team members, and the HR team. Following the candidate's offer acceptance, it's a great time for the hiring manager to consider the question:

*How can I make sure my new team
member gets to a full contribution level as
quickly as possible?*

On-boarding includes being introduced to team members, company culture, and performance objectives. On-boarding generally happens over a period of weeks or months and it may even extend to the first year of employment.

This process has touch-points throughout where the new team member and hiring manager can be sure each is aware of how the team member is acclimating.

On-boarding should have some employee-driven aspects where the new team member has an opportunity to engage with others to learn about their role, how their role fits into the company, who they will interact with, and how they can contribute value to the business.

Performance management

Sometimes we confuse managing performance with having a robust strategy for administering this process for the company. Managing performance is simple. You talk to your employees about what they're achieving and what they aren't, and you establish objectives to do something differently going forward. Creating a performance management system is more complicated.

You don't need a complicated process to effectively manage performance.

You need to keep it simple.

You also don't need a costly system. You need to have an established practice that you're going to have frequent conversations about what's happening in your organization. The more frequent the conversations, the shorter they will be. The more frequent the conversations are, the less likely your managers will have to handle performance deficiencies. The more frequent the conversations are, the more engaged your managers and employees will feel about their work.

As an HR professional I think I'm supposed to tell you that performance management is the most critical thing you can do for your business. Okay, so I will tell you that's the case. But I will not tell you that it needs to be a laborious process. Because here's the thing – I've been the HR person who has had to tell her managers that performance management is a long, drawn out process with levels of documentation and review. I don't believe that to be the case anymore. Here's how simple it can be.

At a minimum, each manager and employee will have a discussion on a quarterly basis. This meeting will be scheduled for 20 minutes. Prior to the meeting, the employee will think of two things he/she's accomplished that quarter and one thing that needs to be worked on in the coming quarter.

The manager will do the same thing (write two accomplishments and one outstanding issue.) During the 20-minute discussion, the manager and employee compare notes and create a game plan.

The next quarter, the meeting is scheduled for 30 minutes. The first 10 minutes reviews the work from the previous quarter and the last 20 minutes the team discusses plans for the coming quarter.

It's that simple. 30 minutes each quarter. Each person has a pre-written outline coming into the meeting. Each person has a document to sign off on at the end of the meeting. That's it.

If you had a simple plan like that – wouldn't it mean so much more to your team than annual performance meetings? No one remembers what they did last week let alone what they did 10 months ago!

Keep it simple.

OperamHR.com/book

Click on the ENGAGE section and enter code: SimpleHR

Look for:
12 Week Goals and Engagement Tracking
Orientation – Personnel File Checklist
Orientation – Hiring Manager Checklist
On-Boarding – First 60 Days

Engagement Point #4 – Am I rewarded and recognized for my contributions?

Rewards and recognition have taken on different expressions through the years. Gold watches and plaques at milestone anniversaries are rarely handed out by companies anymore. And often employee bonuses are the first thing slashed from an operating budget in lean years at companies – never to return in the successful years.

The disappearance of these rewards and recognition programs have left the modern employee feeling as though their employer doesn't really care about them. Intentional or otherwise, the absence of rewards and recognition give the impression to employees that companies of today are all about themselves and not about the employee.

It doesn't have to be that way. There are simple programs that can be implemented to make employees feel rewarded and recognized for their great efforts. These programs don't have to cost the company thousands of dollars and they don't have to be complex. But they should reflect the culture you're trying to cultivate at your company. I don't believe in a one-size-fits-all approach for rewards programs. Nonetheless, here are some thoughts:

Compensation

Face it, pay is the reason most people work so it's a personal topic to your employees. Compensation challenges are some of the most difficult to sort out at a company. Annual raises – who gets them, why should employees receive increases, and can the business afford them? Or merit increases based on performance evaluations – what if you don't even do performance evaluations? These challenges are some that every company faces at one point or another.

Pay is one piece of the 4 Steps of Engagement at your company. Considering your company's culture is so important when you think about adjusting pay. Any decision you make should relate to your culture. Your decisions will certainly impact your culture. That doesn't mean if your business can afford generous increases you will have very satisfied employees who rush into work and volunteer for every complex project in the company. It certainly can help encourage that type of behavior but it's only one piece of the culture puzzle. Alternatively, if your business is going through a tough time and cannot afford increases, the way you handle the communication to employees is key to keeping them engaged and interested in staying with your company.

How would you want a conversation about your own pay to occur between you and your manager?

Having honest conversations with employees about their performance, about the status of the business, and about their pay can go a long way in making employees feel like they are valued.

Think about how you would want a conversation about your own pay to occur between you and your manager. No matter what level you hold at a company, you would feel more comfortable and confident if you heard the honest story.

Some of you reading this may work for publicly traded companies, and so you have to be sensitive to the amount of information shared openly within the company. That's a very real concern – but it doesn't mean you can't speak honestly about someone's personal performance, about why an increase was determined for someone, and about how the business determined a budget for increases in the upcoming year.

Depending on your role, you are in a position to make pay decisions or recommend pay changes for your team members. You might not be in a position to determine a budget or make final pay approvals. However, *you* can control the message given to your team – about a performance review or a pay change. *You* are in control of the way the message is delivered to your team. And *you* are in control of the way you shape the culture of your team and the business as a whole. Planning and communication can help keep your employees feeling engaged and respected throughout the process.

Recognition

Pizza parties and plaques on the wall are ways to celebrate wins and accomplishments in the organization. They may seem old fashioned but some employees might see it as a simple way to gather, build community, and have common ground among each other. The manner in which you recognize achievements can vary across companies and I think its approach should reflect a sensitivity to your culture. Take the time to investigate this.

What recognition programs have you used at the company in the past?

_____

_____

_____

Did these programs work well or fall flat?

_____

_____

Why do you think these programs worked well or didn't?

_____

_____

Who designed these programs? Leadership or staff members?

_____

When you consider a recognition program, it might be helpful to get the input of team members. After all, they're the people who will be recognized or rewarded for their performance. You can have a poll that selects the type of rewards that will be offered. You can create a committee that handles these decisions. Whatever makes sense for your business is the approach you should take.

Because I like to help you take action – simple, quick, impactful actions – list out the following ways you will create rewards and recognition for your team.

What are the 2 – 3 things you'd like to recognize? Options could be milestone anniversaries, birthdays, project management achievement, profit growth for the company, etc.

1. _____

_____

2. _____

_____

3. _____

_____

How would you like to reward these achievements?

_____

_____

_____

_____

When will you implement the first recognition program?

_____

_____

For additional tactics on engagement including 12 simple tips on engaging to maximize performance, recognition, and rewards, visit OperamHR.com/book

Click on the ENGAGE section and enter code: SimpleHR

Look for:
Engage – 12 Helpful Tips

Trust

Why should your employees trust you?

Let's turn "what's in it for me" back to the employer to answer this question. You need employees to trust you for a laundry list of reasons but here are a few to help get you thinking.

Employees who have trust in the company will tell you what's really happening in the business. They'll be honest with you about what's working and what isn't. But more importantly, they will likely be engaged enough to help be a solution to the problems instead of just voicing frustrations. The resolution of those types of issues can have real, hard dollar returns to your business.

Employees who do not trust the company are perhaps fearful of retaliation or that no one will listen to their concerns. If this is happening to your employees, it likely will result in a general *laissez faire* attitude that permeates your business.

How do you show your trust?

In any relationship there are signals you can read, ignore, or be oblivious to. Perhaps you've heard this from a spouse or a friend – *hint hint!* Your work relationships send signals, too.

Frequently asking for more to do. Interest in attending additional meetings or travel. Showing up early or staying late. These are signals that show engagement.

Lack of response. Frequent absences. Delays in meeting objectives. These are all signals of a different kind. The way you respond to these signals shows a level of your own engagement and your own trust in the employee.

My experience with the toughest manager I ever had was a mantra of "Trust but Verify." While I understood what he meant, when I looked back on it he didn't actually trust me. He did. But he didn't. It's the same as someone saying, "I'll give you enough rope... but you might end up hanging from it." That's not really showing trust either.

"I'll give you enough rope ... but you might end up hanging from it."

The way you show trust is by offering the most training needed for someone to be successful and then challenging them to the tasks related to that training. Assigning them to projects you feel confident they can handle and following up to check in on progress. Giving people the access to other team members or vendors to gather data or research to make the best possible decisions for your company. And if you're really in the mode of trust, allowing people to determine their schedule or a work-from-home arrangement will indicate trust.

Just like your personal relationships, you won't come into trust overnight. You shouldn't. But keep an open mind to the amount of work and access you're giving to your employees. Allow them some space to make decisions and have success. Allow them space to make mistakes and counsel them so it doesn't happen again. They will likely thank you for it by asking for more, trying harder, and helping others.

How will employees show their trust?

I mentioned before that employees who are engaged and trust you will be more likely to voice their opinions and contribute to process improvements. They may also be inclined to contribute to something higher on your priority list. Employees who have trust in a company are more likely to feel comfortable fulfilling the company's (true) obligations of compliance under the law. It's a vulnerable position for employees to take the risk of blowing the whistle on a direct manager or executive. Think about and appreciate the tough position your employees are in when making those kinds of statements about the company's leaders.

So how do you help employees understand why they should trust the company? The responsibility falls on the shoulders of the company and its leaders.

Are corporate secrets destroying your company?

You've read the papers. A huge corporation has a catastrophic PR nightmare because something inappropriate was happening seemingly right under the noses of the executives. Outrageous! Penalties and lawsuits abound following the scandal. Negative media haunts the company.

Inevitably the questions are asked – Who knew about these issues? How could this type of thing go on without anyone knowing? Did the company have a confidential method of reporting these issues?

All logical questions after the facts come to light. But what about proactive approaches? How do you get more employees to speak up?

Think about how vulnerable it can feel for an employee to acknowledge that what they are witnessing is wrong. Think about how difficult it can be for an employee to consider losing their job, their livelihood, and their personal reputation if they voice their concerns. It's an incredibly difficult proposition for an employee.

Regardless of confidential methods of reporting impropriety, employees can still feel reluctant to acknowledge wrong doing – particularly of the wrong-doers are in superior positions to their own.

Actions. Actions speak louder than words, than training sessions, or websites. Those things are necessary too, but don't fool yourself into thinking that those things alone will encourage your employees to speak up. Here are some examples of small changes with big impact:

- Walking around to your team members' offices and work areas.
- Talking to employees in casual settings as often as there are formal meetings.
- Eating or socializing together in small groups not just in large, all-company settings.

All of these steps go toward building trust with employees so they will feel more comfortable voicing concerns. Successful CEOs who've implemented one or two of these activities have a noticeable impact in their knowledge of the business, the employee's response to their availability, and a change in the middle levels of management to have access to employee thoughts and contributions.

Be accessible. Ask questions.

Access to information and hearing directly from employees can pull the proverbial veil from the secrets that underlie most businesses. Want to know why product management doesn't seem to have an understanding of the voice of your customers? Maybe there is an undercurrent of negativity in that department that prevents people from discussing external feedback on products or services. Did you see a statistic that customer service isn't responding to customer issues quickly? There might be a tool the team is missing – but how would you know if you never visit their department or see their workspace?

These are powerful changes for you to make – and they're relatively small changes for a big impact.

The pitfalls of distrust

Did you read the articles in 2016 about a sexual harassment case at Fox News Corporation?

After that story broke, I posted a link to the article on my LinkedIn page as well as my company's Facebook page. LinkedIn didn't get much response or activity. My Facebook post though – whoa! I have to tell you that I have given anti-harassment and anti-discrimination training many times during my career. I try to make the examples a little funny so people don't completely check out during the presentation of what can be – let's face it – dry material. But now I have a whole new set of examples to give from the responses I got on Facebook.

So what do you think? Are secrets destroying your company's culture?

The responses I read on Facebook were raw and honest. Social media is our opportunity to vent exactly what we think – even though it's not even close to being anonymous. The responses went from "Of course this case is harassment!" to "She's old and got fired so now she's suing!" to "Way to play the woman card!"

These responses were not surprising. Definitely interesting and somewhat disappointing.

A couple of thoughts about secrets. People having affairs or alleging affairs or inappropriate relationships in the workplace can be distracting to the forward progress of the organization. Whether these relationships are kept in secret or not, these interpersonal relationships tend to disrupt the natural flow of a team. Are they always a form of harassment? Not always. But typically they impact the culture of the organization.

Company executives or ethics officers are usually the last to know about theft or fraud. These activities are kept as a secret from leadership but often employees know it is happening. It's a secret everyone is forced to keep until the issue bubbles to the surface. In the meantime the secrets negatively impact the culture of the organization.

All of this got me thinking. What are the real opinions of people who work at companies?

In training sessions people are generally polite. They might chuckle at a few jokes, they might answer a few questions here and there, but what are they really thinking? Do they have enough trust to voice their real opinions? I haven't seen brutal honesty often in the workplace and certainly not as often as I have seen on social media. But if people really believe the things they write in social media and those same people work at your company, are their real beliefs the secrets that tread just under the surface of your company's culture? Are those the secrets that bubble up and cause disruptions to teamwork and goal achievements and overall culture?

I don't have an answer to any of these questions. But you should think about them and answer honestly. If you are honest with yourself and these challenges exist in your company, you may have some work to do. Don't shy away from it. Culture issues happen at all companies of all sizes at any given time. It can be a combination of factors. What you have control over is the ability to resolve the issues and improve your culture.

What can you do?

So let's say you're not a CEO. Maybe you're not a people manager. Can you learn from this? Can you implement any of these tactics? Sure you can. Here's a list of ideas to get you started:

- Schedule a 30-minute block of time twice per week to visit your team members. Ask questions that relate to the employee's interests, needs, or goals. Does the employee have an interest in attending training? Has the employee recently joined a project team? If so, what's his/her impression of the project team?
- If you're a department or project manager, ask project members to work in an open project environment.

(Take over a conference room or set up an open work space in your office.) Explain to the team that you'll be visiting to contribute as often as you will to evaluate progress. Oh, and actually go to those meetings after you commit to doing so.

- Spend 10 minutes each week visiting a different department. Talk with a counterpart in other departments and learn about what it is they're working on. Who knows? You might have a lot more in common than you think!

- Have a team lunch. It can be once a month or once a quarter. In addition to bringing in lunch, ask employees to bring a topic to the table for discussion. The topic can be related to a work project, training, recently read article, or brainstorming idea.

- Prior to annual budget review, solicit input from your team. Ask them, "If you had the opportunity to create our budget next year, what would you include / what would you cut?"

These ideas build on the idea of an office-less CEO and focus on having engaging business conversations with employees and colleagues. It's these little things that lead to better employee engagement.

Engagement – that's the key to better profitability, longevity and a thriving business.

For more information on how to effectively engage your team, visit OperamHR.com/book

Click on the ENGAGE section and enter code: SimpleHR

Look for:
Engage – 12 Simple Tips

Challenge your thinking

I read an article in *The Atlantic* about "America's fantasy of a 4-day work week." Think through it with me... Imagine a world where Mondays are good days... *ahhhhh...*

> "For the foreseeable future, the 32-hour fantasy will remain a quirk and a perk – a way for small, forward-thinking companies in knowledge industries to compete with their more powerful rivals for talented employees."
> *– Brigid Schulte, The Washington Post, February 2015*

In all seriousness, the article from *The Atlantic* highlights a company called Treehouse that has challenged the idea of a traditional 40-hour work week where employees work 5 days a week. This company encourages 32 hours per week (four 8-hour days). And they don't have a loss of productivity. They haven't lost out on growth or revenue. They've flourished because employees have choice, balance between work and home, and feel rested between work weeks.

I'm not sure if every business can accommodate a 32-hour work week without carefully reviewing required headcount and budgetary concerns. But I think it's possible to think about the traditional work week differently.

Here are some ideas:

Could you populate your team with people who work less than 40 hours? Perhaps they are stay-at-home parents who want to work 9a-3p during the school year, or other qualified candidates who may not be able to work 8 hours per day.

In the summer, could you offer employees the ability to flex their start and end times so they can spend more time outside or with family?

Could you offer employees the ability to work four 10-hour days? (Ensuring your team has overlap on three core days per week – some have Monday off, some have Friday off.)

This goes back to the "What's in it for Me?" mentality that most employees will continually have at your company. That mentality doesn't change. In fact, it evolves. That means your way of thinking will continually need to evolve. The programs you created in Year 1 or 10 or 50 of your business will not hold up for more than 5 or 10 years after you establish them. You have to keep in touch with the needs of your workforce and contemporary practices both inside and outside of your industry.

The "firm 40" hour work week

How many hours of work per week do you average? Is it around 40? Is it inevitably well over 40, which by the laws of averages means you're putting in well over 50 hours most weeks?

How many hours on average do you think your team members are working? Not just what they're reporting to you that they're working but actual time? Like the emails after hours. The checking in on weekends. The "I'm bored at my child's soccer game so I'll just catch up on a few things before Monday..."

There is a company in Michigan that's implemented a new rule. They tell employees, "You give us 40 hours and you keep the rest."

A firm 40-hour work week. Really?!

I almost feel badly about my surprise and skepticism when I read this article in The Wall Street Journal. I've been working for over 20 years in professional-level roles where overtime is the company's expectation. Quite frankly, it's my expectation that I work closer to 50 hours each week than 40. (Did I mention domestic and global travel during most of my career? Let's not go there. But you get the picture.)

Why is that the expectation? Is it self-imposed because we think it will get us ahead of competition? Is it an unwritten expectation from managers?

As you reflect on your career, do you remember similar situations? If so, think about the expectations you as a leader are setting for your team members. Really think about it.

I'll challenge you to this. Call a team meeting and tell your team to read the *WSJ* "Firm 40" article. Then ask them to brainstorm how this approach could be implemented.

Where would you start to tear apart the expectations of the tireless grind?

How would everything get done if you had 40 hours per person instead of 40+?

I bet you'll find similar actions as United Shore Financial Services: employees policing each other's work hours, and contributing to each other's projects.

Follow-through is key

I am a big believer in: Communication, Development, and Follow-through.

Follow-through is key to your success and that's not a gimmick or a line I'm feeding you. You lose credibility when you say you're going to do something and don't follow through with it.

Let's say you started off the year with goals and objectives and forgot to check in with your team about their progress. Let's say it's July and you didn't set goals at the beginning of the year at all.

What are you going to do?

You're going to start doing all of that NOW. Your employees will thank you no matter what if you set an objective and follow through with it. It doesn't matter what month of the year it happens. What matters is that it *does happen*. If you started something and didn't get around to completing it, now is your chance to make good on those commitments to yourself and others.

- If you made a New Year's resolution but didn't follow through – do it now.
- If you had plans to create goals for this year but didn't – do it now.
- If you met with your team earlier this month to enlist their help with achieving a goal – follow up now.
- If you didn't show appreciation for your team members this month – do it now.

Don't feel overwhelmed by this list. You don't have to do it all! Do one of these things. Just one. Just ONE! Make changes that are manageable, not something that causes you more frustrations.

Open your eyes to the stressors of your business

Stress and depression are killers. That's right, killers.

I've given you so many tips and tools and reflective exercises you could be feeling very overwhelmed right now. Maybe you even put the book down and decided that you're done with this! Keep in mind, that could be how your team members feel when they are confronted with the list of tasks they have to complete. Or if they feel like they aren't meeting your objectives.

Stress and depression are killers.

I would encourage you to take the issues of stress and depression in the workplace seriously. If you think that you or your team members can get through it on your own, chances are you're wrong. You'll learn about the stressors of your teams when you start walking around the offices and asking questions. Team stress will become abundantly clear to you. Don't let that scare you away from detecting it and dealing with it! It may cause you stress, and I'm sensitive to that with your own health. But the leader is sometimes the only one who can make changes to help ease the stress of the team.

Here are some strategies to assist you:

1) Encourage team members to take a break during the day. Make sure they feel like they can walk away from their desks, work stations, or assembly lines 1-2 times per day. If they're offered scheduled breaks – make sure they take them! If you have control of your day, set an appointment on your calendar to walk away even if it's just for 5 minutes.

2) Talk about workload. Even if you're scared to the point that the conversation alone stresses you out – you have to talk about your workload. Employees may not go to their

managers first. Encourage them to talk with colleagues in their department or someone in another department. Sometimes getting frustrations out in the open is a good stress reliever. Make sure there is a way to convey the stress to someone who can help alleviate it so the conversation has a benefit and doesn't turn into a toxic b*tch session! There needs to be an outcome.

3) Eat. I'm not even going to write "eat well" because if you're so stressed out, you may not even be eating at all. Depression can set in if you let stress take away your basic needs. That can include remembering to eat and drink water. Make sure you eat and drink throughout the day.

4) Eat well. Okay, now I'll write this. Eating well gives your body and mind the nutrients needed to fire on all cylinders. If you put cheap gas in your car it will perform well only to a point. Same thing for your body. Sometimes a little spinach or an apple can get your mind where you need it to be.

Do not let stress take over your life. And be mindful that it might be taking over the lives of your team members. Growing businesses especially are sometimes so focused on the goals that they don't take time for a break. I lived with stress and depression for long periods of time and got way too caught up in a bad spiral of life. I relied on people to help me get through it. So can you. So can your employees.

Think about an Employee Assistance Program that can support you and your team. There is probably an EAP in your area, and the expenses are typically incurred when your employees utilize the services. It could be a great benefit you offer with little overall cost. But offering the benefit may be what your employees need to hear to let them know you care about their wellbeing.

The guilt around vacation time

We covered this earlier but it's worth reminding you. Americans are workaholics. It's been proven in study after study. We are a dedicated bunch of people committed to productivity and achievement at our careers. I take pride in my work and many of you do, too.

But time is ticking in this calendar year to take vacation. Time away.

Don't feel guilty about vacation time. And don't make your employees feel guilty about it either. You need to use the time off and so do they!

Does any of this ring true to you?!

#1 reason I don't take time off is because I work on vacation and I don't enjoy it.

#2 reason I don't take time off is I have too much to do and I'd be thinking about work the whole time I'm off.

#3 reason I don't take time off is I feel like I'll let my team members down if I'm not at the meeting next week.

We can allow the course of business to trump our need to take a break. It's very easy to do that. But this mindset change starts by behavior at the top. If you take time off, your employees will feel more confident in doing it too. It may not be easy to change to that behavior. But really, what's your challenge with taking time off?

"Engagement" can feel like a state of nirvana that no company can every fully achieve.

---

12 Engagement Tips

Engagement is becoming an all too often used catch phrase and can feel like a state of nirvana that no company can ever fully achieve. Look, take this step by step. Add in one or two of the tactics or ideas presented in this section of the book. Don't try to do all of it in one fell swoop! That's completely unrealistic and you and the team will be disappointed when you don't achieve any of the goals.

Keep your engagement tactics simple. Don't overcomplicate the necessities and keep these simple rules in mind:

Engagement
Greater levels of engagement will result if the team members understand how they can directly contribute to the success of the company and how they will be rewarded or recognized for achievements.

What's in it for me?
If you want someone to give you more, talk with them about the value they bring and the value the project brings to them – not just how their efforts will benefit the company.

Goals
Does your team know the goals of a project and how it fits into the achievement of the company's goals? You have a greater chance for engagement if the team understands how individual, team, and corporate goals align.

Recognition
People make great strides every day. Talk with employees about their individual efforts or contributions to the team. Remember to recognize the achievements of each person.

Say Thank You!
The simplest way to make someone feel as though they are contributing is to say thank you for a job well done. Schedule

one day per week when you send at least one thank you to a team member.

Follow-through

You can have the best intentions but if you don't follow through, no one will feel committed or engaged. If you say that you are committed to a project or your team, then follow through with actions.

Get employees involved

Employees like to be involved with planning and decision making. Take the opportunity to solicit input and delegate ownership to create higher levels of engagement.

Be Visible

Spend time visiting with employees to learn their contributions, concerns and ideas. Schedule 30 minutes this week to meet with a team member and learn about her goals and how you can work better together.

Check in often

When was the last time you checked in with your team? Ask these three things:

- What were the goals we last set?
- What work has been done to accomplish the goal?
- What's left to achieve?

Team meetings

Have you had a team meeting recently? Make sure you follow through on the topics and ideas raised during those meetings.

Rewards

It's the small things. A lunch. A cup of coffee. An extra long lunch break. Give one of these things to your team this week.

Talk to each other

Do you have 30 minutes this week to talk to your team? Schedule it now. Do it this week. Do it every week.

COMPLY

Staying Compliant

I'm generally not an advocate of scare tactics when it comes to encouraging business owners to comply with certain laws. But let's face it —mistakes can sometimes be incredibly costly. The price tag isn't the big deal though, really. It's the compounding issues that will result if you're not compliant. The same is true with your taxes. You can sneak through one loophole but another will catch you.

This section is written to outline common compliance issues I often encounter with my clients. It's not an all-encompassing list but it's a good start. Chances are if my clients experience these pitfalls so do you.

Your $250,000 problem

One of the obstacles I come up against with clients is to quantify the risk that may be lurking in their business. It is one thing to say that I believe there is a potential for risk, but often it's hard to express how great that risk may be. This example is a good one to help you get perspective on the dollars and cents costs to the business for noncompliant practices.

I met with a human resources colleague who told me about a situation he encountered at a former employer. This colleague was an HR Manager at a reputable company – reputable in the standpoint that its vendors and customers recognized them as a leader in the industry.

Their employees, however, didn't view the company as being reputable.

When this colleague joined the company as an HR Manager he had a cold reception from the supervisors and employees. This isn't all that uncommon for an HR Manager – we are sometimes known as the company's "police force" or "the principal's office." But my friend's reception was even colder than usual. No one seemed comfortable to talk about business practices. So he started digging into the data. When he looked at payroll he sensed there was an unusually low overtime cost compared to what he saw with a parking lot full of employees' cars 6 days a week. He also noticed that vacation accrual compared to payout was off-balance.

This company had a $250,000 problem.
And you might have this problem, too.

Very quickly my colleague uncovered why people didn't want to open up to him and why the company had lingering issues.

The industry this business operated in was tough. Thin margins. Global competition. Dying technology. The finance and operations leaders asked the employees to "pick up the tab," so to speak, with some of the margin numbers they needed to make up after the business lost a major contract. They cut corners with overtime pay and didn't grant paid time off.

These are the things my colleague looked for. And it's what every Department of Labor auditor will look for as well. The issues are easy to find, but here's a list in case you want to do a self-audit.

1) Do you use paper time sheets? If you're still using paper to track worked hours there are risks to this process. Hours can be forged. Payroll processing takes longer. And supervisors can pressure employees to cut their hours to prevent overtime pay. Consider using an electronic method. There are apps on phones that can be used at a much lower cost than full-blown time keeping and HRIS. Find the best system for you, but here are a few ideas:

- TSheets.com
- Toggl.com
- Capterra.com
- Timekamp

A view of the Toggl dashboard

2) Does your time clock round-up or down? It's hard to calculate payroll in real time minutes and fractions of dollars. Many companies will establish a rule that time is rounded up or down depending on when someone clocks in or out. *This is the $250,000 problem* my colleague encountered at his former employer. His employer at the time set up the time clock to round down to the closest 15 minutes if the person clocked in or out late. So if someone worked until 4:12 and clocked out at 4:14, the clock was set to show 4:00 as the clocked out time, docking the employee 14 minutes of pay. This type of thing happened for the 260 hourly employees working at the company.

And it triggered $250,000 in penalties for violating wage and hour laws in their state.

3) Do your employees and supervisors sign time sheets before payroll is processed? Most states differ on the exact language but most agree that employees and supervisors BOTH should confirm the hours worked each week and sign off on approval before payroll is processed. This is a good practice to implement if you're not doing so already.

Timekeeping and payroll are complex processes for any business. Your company's practices may need to be different from another company's. But think about some of the aforementioned pitfalls my colleague ran into. Understand that every company has some issues with its timekeeping and payroll practices. But there are ways you can fix them. Take the right steps now before you are hit with an audit from the Department of Labor or other government agency!

P.S. You might imagine it was an employee who notified the state Wage and Hour office about the company's mismanagement of timekeeping and payroll practices. This company has only 40 people working for it now. **Don't let this happen to you!**

What is the FLSA?

I field so many questions about the Fair Labor Standards Act (FLSA) regulations. It's an old law that was created at a time when there were not very many standards for U.S. workers. Working conditions were unsafe. Children were employed by the hundreds. There were no regulations about the maximum number of hours people could work, or giving them breaks during the day or between shifts. And there were no regulations about how people were paid. The FLSA was established in 1938 and established minimum wage, overtime pay, recordkeeping, and child labor standards affecting full-time and part-time workers in the private sector and in Federal, State, and local governments.

A few key elements of this law that every business owner should know:

Salary Threshold

The current wage threshold is $455 per week. What this means is anyone who earns less than $455 per week is eligible to earn overtime. It doesn't matter what their job duties are. The salary threshold is the first factor to review.

Exemption status

It will be easier if you start by thinking about all employees as being eligible to earn overtime, then work backward from there. That's because of something called Exemption Status. There are five exemption categories: Executive, Administrative, Professional, Computer, and Outside Sales. To determine if a position is exempt from earning overtime, there are a few important questions that must be answered. Each category has a certain list of questions. Below is a summary of them.

- Does the person meet a weekly salary threshold (see above)?
- Do the employee's duties involve directing and managing subordinate employees independently?

- Do the employee's primary duties involve office or non-manual work directly related to the management or general business operations of the employer?

Highly Compensated Employees (HCE)

If someone earns more than a certain amount in a tax year, this position is considered to be highly compensated and the individual is not eligible to earn overtime wages.

PLEASE NOTE: This limit is different than the limit the IRS uses to determine HCE status for pension or retirement savings programs.

Much of the FLSA is out of date for today's working standards. It doesn't address modern working issues like mobile phones, a 24/7 working world, and I think we could all agree that $455 per week is not a "living wage" anymore. However, any changes to the law impacts so many elements of American business and American workers, most congressional sessions have decided to leave well enough alone, so to speak. In 2016 the Obama Administration took a strong stand that overtime regulations and exemptions should be adjusted dramatically. Fortunately cooler heads prevailed – in the Federal Court of Eastern Texas – and the changes were postponed and virtually abandoned following the election of the next administration.

There was so much talk at that time about how businesses were going to afford the changes to the FLSA standards.

Here's the thing, most of my clients are violating the existing regulations.

Because overtime can seem costly, many businesses violate existing regulations. And YOU may be, too. Here are some ways to know if you're violating the basic principles of the FLSA.

Common pitfalls of FLSA

1. If you consider all employees to be "salaried" without regard to the work they do or the wage they earn, you are likely in violation of the existing standards.
2. If you sign off on time sheets that show "8 A.M. − 5 P.M." as the hours worked for every day in your pay cycles, you are likely in violation of the existing standards.
3. If you know people at your company work through their unpaid lunch or unpaid breaks and you allow that behavior to occur, you are likely in violation of the existing standards.

This type of activity happened in every corporation I worked for and it happens with most of my clients. Companies large and small are guilty of this behavior.

Why does it happen so often?

Well, first of all it's difficult to track employee's time worked particularly with the advent of the 24/7 global economy, smart phones, and online access no matter where you are in the world. Second, when you consider telling a dedicated employee that they need to stop working because you don't want to pay them overtime, it's likely a statement you don't want to make and the employee doesn't want to hear it. Talk about a way to disengage someone quickly – that's a good way to do it!

You don't have room for excuses anymore.

The thing is, you don't have any room for excuses. If you're in violation today you'll be in violation in the future. You need to take action now. Here are some ideas.

Think about FLSA compliance like this: everyone is entitled to earning overtime for hours worked beyond 40 hours per week unless you can prove an exemption to the overtime pay. So if you start with the mindset that everyone is eligible for overtime, then you can more easily back into which positions should be identified as exempt from earning overtime.

Once you identify which positions should be paid overtime, then it's time to look at who may not be paid as often as they need to be. If there are a group of people who frequently work through their lunches or breaks or work late into the evening, it's time to have a conversation with them. This is a positive employee relations conversation as much as it is about overtime compliance so go about the conversation in that manner. Talk with the group or individuals about why they are working more than the standard day. Get to know the reasons and create solutions from there. Start with a focus on the individual's needs and then move on to how their needs can be accommodated by the business. You may not be able to accommodate their needs completely but having the conversation with them first will go a long way!

Timesheets are your friend.
Timesheets are your enemy.

Auditors love to look at timesheets when they come to your company to investigate infractions. The accuracy of timesheets is a top way to uncover not only issues with pay practices but it's usually the Pandora's Box for an auditor. How often do you think your employees actually work a standard day, like 8 A.M. – 5 P.M. every single day? There are days when they will come in early or late, take a longer lunch, or leave early or late. There are days when employees might check email at home or attend a conference or an event on behalf of the company. Are all of those times being recorded accurately? That's what an auditor from the Department of

Labor is going to be looking for. They won't believe you when you say that everyone works a standard day from 8 A.M. – 5 P.M. The onus is on you to defend your timesheets. Can you do that easily? No way! Saying that "Timekeeping is really hard" isn't an excuse that's going to work for you. Believe me. I've lived through this before.

Shall we break for lunch?

Let's tackle one of the toughest issues with pay compliance – people eating lunch or snacks at their desks during unpaid lunch or breaks. It's really, really difficult to regulate this in your company unless you have a designated warden patrolling people's work areas. And if that's your culture – have at it! But if you're like most employers you are not encouraging people to tell on each other for being dedicated. And that's what we are typically talking about here.

People who work through unpaid breaks are doing so because they are either dedicated to their employer or it means something to them to get their work done and get it done well. You don't want to turn off that level of dedication! And you don't have to if you decide to pay people when they work through their lunch or breaks. What if you modified your lunch and break schedule to read something like:

> "We believe people need breaks throughout their day. You need to walk away from your work space for at least 30 minutes for lunch and at least 10 minutes in the morning or afternoon. Because we believe in this for your mental and physical health, you cannot work during that time and you will not be paid for that time. We would like it if you took even more time as an unpaid break – up to 60 minutes at lunch and 10 minutes in the morning and the afternoon. But we understand if you feel like you need to get projects done or handle customer issues."

The penalties are real for noncompliance. Here's a recent example in Ohio where the courts decided that because the employee self-identified her time in great detail but submitted only 40 hours per week *and* there was no manager oversight to make corrections, she was paid only straight time for hours. Well she figured out she was likely eligible for overtime pay since her hiring in 2010 so she filed a claim for back wages.

Guess what? She won.

The court went on to say that the employer had the responsibility for reviewing the timesheets, making changes as necessary and ensuring people are paid for all the hours they work. Further, the employer has to plan for overtime costs in the annual budget of the business.

You have no more excuses. It's time to get into compliance.

Why is pay transparency such a big deal?

If you've been reading the book straight through, you've read this phrase a few times "employment-value proposition." The way you discuss pay – meaning pay decisions and pay strategies around cost of living adjustments, merit increase, promotions, and recruiting – the transparency of this information is part of your employment-value proposition and impacts your company's culture and its compliance.

Beyond that, pay transparency is part of the law.

There are more stringent requirements for companies to have clear pay transparency under the NLRA, and as a recent step by the Office of Federal Contract Compliance Programs OFCCP (www.dol.gov/ofccp), these measures help ensure that employees understand how their pay is determined and how one person's pay compares to others. The National Labor Relations Act (NLRA) also has amendments related to allowing employees to discuss their pay without threat of discipline or termination by the employer. This is true even if you are a non-union employer.

Why is this happening?

Equal pay has received press for many years since the passing of the Equal Pay Act of 1963 and its revisions via Lilly Ledbetter Fair Pay Restoration Act of 2009.

No employer having employees subject to any provisions of this section shall discriminate, within any establishment in which such employees are employed, between employees on the basis of sex

– Equal Pay Act of 1963

The OFCCP has long been interested in looking at creating diverse work forces at companies. As time has gone on it's followed along the course of action with other federal laws to identify equal pay as an important factor among protected classes:

- Age
- Disability
- Equal Pay/Compensation
- Genetic Information
- Harassment
- National Origin
- Pregnancy
- Race/Color
- Religion
- Retaliation
- Sex
- Sexual Harassment

On September 10, 2015, the OFCCP released its final "Pay Transparency" rule designed to promote pay transparency and eliminate the wage gap between females and males and minorities and non-minorities. OFCCP believes the rule "provides a critical tool to encourage pay transparency, so workers have a potential way of discovering violations of equal pay laws and can seek appropriate remedies."

A culture of secrecy prevents employees from finding out if they are being discriminated against in time to act on it.

— OFCCP Rule on Pay Transparency

What does this mean for you?

At this time the rule applies to companies which must comply with OFCCP regulations, and for those companies the rule went into effect for any contract entered into on or after January 11, 2016. Those companies have to implement a number of processes to achieve compliance with the new rule.

Get ready, things are about to change

Even if your company does not have government contractor status or compliance requirements, there are things you can do to ensure you have pay transparency. File this in your mind as *things are about to change.*

When the OFCCP outlines a change for federal contractors, usually companies outside of that sector see changes, too. Can you start being pro-active? Sure you can. Here are some ideas:

- Evaluate your pay practices. Are they based on market data? How recent is that market data? Do you need to refresh your approach?
- Compare the people who sit in the same job title or department who have relatively similar job responsibilities and scope. Do you have job descriptions for these jobs? If not, write them and communicate the description to the employee.
- For the same group of people, look at each person's skills, experience, and training. Are the pay differences between each person based on higher/lower skill sets? If not, consider making some changes.

Handbook

Ahhh... the employee handbook... loathed by HR people and employees alike. It's the rule book. It's the set of all things firm and focused at our company. Or is it?

I've found that the handbooks at my former employers and some of my clients were outdated and really didn't reflect the way the company did business with its employees. There were rules and regulations outlined in the handbook but ultimately each situation impacted the way the employer chose outcomes.

A handbook is an agreement with your employees on how you're going to do business together.

I view handbooks as a communication tool. The employer outlines all the benefits that will be offered to employees. In turn, the employer has certain expectations of employees in order to receive those benefits. It seems simple enough, right?

You'll find that as your business starts, evolves, and matures, the tone of your handbook and the required elements in it will change over time. And it should. Contracts you put in place with suppliers and customers will evolve over time, too – so shouldn't the agreement you have with your employees also evolve?

As your business becomes more successful you'll have the ability to afford more robust benefits programs including insurance and paid time off; you'll be able to be more or less lax in attendance or work from home policies; and you'll have the benefit of hindsight on what approaches have worked in the past and what will be ideal for your future. I think you should consider updating your handbook at least every 5 years. If your business is growing fast then you might want to consider adjusting it more frequently.

For a standard table of contents for your employee handbook, visit:
OperamHR.com/book

Click on the COMPLY section and enter code: SimpleHR

Look for:
Comply – Table of Contents

Policies

What are the types of policies you should include in your handbook? Here are a few ideas, but if you'd like a longer list, contact me and we can talk about what's truly needed for your business, its industry, and the size of your company.

I don't believe in giving templates for something as individual as a handbook, but we can collaborate on the ideas together. Here are some ideas to get you started:

Welcome

Introduction / History of the Company

Employment-related topics

    Introductory/Probationary period

    Employment of family members

    Re-Hire of former employees

    Non-solicitation

    Employee discipline

    Employee termination

Pay-related matters

    FLSA classifications

    Working hours

    Pay periods and pay dates

    Timekeeping methods

    Deductions from pay

    Direct deposit

Benefits

Employee relations

Equal Employer Opportunity statement

Diversity statement

Anti-harassment/discrimination

Safe workplace

Americans with Disabilities Act compliance

Company policies

Confidentiality and non-disclosure

Ethical conduct

Attendance and punctuality

Dress code

The Alphabet Soup of Employment Laws

FMLA is complicated. Even the acronym is kind of complicated, if you ask me! The Family Medical Leave Act was enacted originally in 1993 and has gone through a number of amendments since then.

FMLA is designed to protect someone's job while they attend to their own medical need or the medical need of an immediate family member. There is a long and winding road that passes through most FMLA cases and typically is not cut and dry, particularly when employee rights under the Americans with Disabilities ACT (ADA) intersect with FMLA.

A few things to keep in mind.

FMLA is not required in all cases. For example, you may work for an employer with less than 50 people at one location (within a certain radius) and so that company does not have to comply with FMLA. But even smaller employers implement FMLA-like policies so pay attention to this example if you fall into either category!

Americans with Disabilities Act (ADA) compliance is required with all private employers.

I was supporting a client recently and wanted to share their scenario. All names have been changed to protect the parties involved (and now suddenly I feel like I'm a TV show writer!). With that, I'll set the stage for you.

A long term, valuable employee named Jake is employed at this company we will call Smoke's Tool Shed. Smoke's has 67 employees who work in one location. Jake was diagnosed with cancer a year ago but he's been working the whole time he's been taking his treatments. Smoke's was willing to work with him if he had to come in late or leave early for his treatments or he wasn't feeling well. Everyone was really proud and supportive of Jake during his treatments.

Recently though, Jake hasn't been feeling well and he's been taking off quite a bit of time. Jake is a tool crib leader which is an important position at Smoke's. Without Jake, other people have to organize the tools and keep track of who borrowed which tools and who hasn't returned them to the crib. People are starting to complain that they can't keep picking up the slack for Jake.

What's a company to do in this situation?

The first question that comes to mind is FMLA because you'll notice it's not referred to in the example. Whether you're "being nice" to an employee or not – or if you're an employee who thinks your company is being really nice to you – you need to get the FMLA paperwork completed at the beginning of this type of illness. It's important to get the clock ticking for FMLA eligibility as well as tracking hours toward what may fluctuate between an intermittent and full time leave. There's no time like the present, so I recommended to my client to get the FMLA paperwork drafted and sent to the employee's physician for completion.

The other thing about FMLA is it's a law designed to protect someone's job. Because every case is different I'm going to write recommendations to consider. We can talk about your approach in more detail if *you contact me directly.*

This case is a test case for a concurrent FMLA and ADA situation. These situations are complicated to handle but it's not impossible. Remember, both laws are designed to protect someone's job.

If Jake needs to have time off because he can't work in his current position *and* he hasn't exhausted his FMLA time for the 12-month eligibility period, then Smoke's will have to keep him in the job he's in and allow him the time off. Smoke's can ask others to pick up his work or hire a temp, but if FMLA isn't exhausted then Jake has to remain the employee "of record" for that particular job under FMLA. And any time he is available to work he has the first right to work that job.

Whether he's exhausted FMLA or not, the ADA's interactive process comes into play. If he medically needs a less physically intense position and you have one to offer, then this is a good approach to have a reasonable accommodation under the ADA.

If Jake has exhausted his FMLA and Smoke's doesn't have a position to move him into, Smoke's still has to go through the interactive process of having a medical review to determine his capabilities.

If you work for an employer that does not offer FMLA, remember that the interactive process under the ADA must still be followed in order to learn about necessary accommodations for the employee.

Leaves of absence – Make the most of these benefits

These are common questions or thoughts that arise when the phrase "leave of absence" is presented to a manager or business owner.

Why would anyone need to take a long leave of absence? Why should I comply with these laws? Disability plans are too expensive for me to implement at my company.

The old-school methodology is that people need to come to work every day and get the job done. In the hectic lives of overworked professionals, working parents and employees who have elder care concerns, long term leaves of absence are taking a new spotlight in the HR world.

These benefits can feel like expenses but there is employee benefit capital that can be earned from implementing these benefit programs. Here are some thoughts for you to consider.

What is a leave of absence?

About.com provides a great definition. A key point is that an employee's employment continues during the term of the leave. Some leaves of absence are provided by employers with limitations in a policy document. Short term leaves of absence include sick time, vacation time, or paid time off and are often accompanied with a wage payment. Longer term leaves of absence are required and defined by law. (See Family Medical Leave Act, or FMLA, at the federal Department of Labor's website.) These types of leaves often do not include a pay element.

Why should you comply with these laws or implement these benefits?

Compliance with the law is important from a financial, operational, and employee relations standpoint of your business. Compliance with the FMLA (or USERRA for military professionals) is relatively easy to implement and administer to full compliance. But beyond the requirement to comply, why should you have these available? I guess I could say, "It's the right thing to do," but that's too simple of an answer. The complexity is in the impact it has on your business, not just the employee.

Leaves of absences provide job protection while someone needs to take a break from work, care for herself, or care for a dependent. That's what is in it for the employee.

What's in it for the employer is:

Minimized recruiting, retention, training: Trained employees return to work at the end of the leave. No need to recruit or train a replacement.

Minimized business disruption: Employees handle the self or family support during a concentrated period of time and return to work without on-going distractions or disruptions.

Maximized employee morale: Employees, managers and team members can have confidence that a needed benefit was provided by the company to an employee.

Expenses of leaves of absence or disability plans

At this point in the U.S. there are few requirements to provide paid leaves of absence. Some states are starting to mandate paid time off for sick time and vacation time. (See Massachusetts Earned Sick Time and California Healthy Workplaces Healthy Families Act of 2014.)

If you don't have plans which provide employees a chance to take any paid time off, you may want to consider implementing one. Some collective bargaining agreements may have a mandate for paid time off in one form or another and with good labor practices in your company, you may choose to offer the same benefits to non-union workers.

These costs are easy to calculate and accrue for with the help of your company's finance team. You may choose to insure your costs with insurance programs like short term or long term disability plans. Those costs too are fairly easy to calculate because your company will typically be charged a monthly premium per participant.

The costs that are more difficult to identify include:

- How many people are likely to utilize a leave of absence program?
- What is the cost to recruit and train an employee to join my company?
- What is the lost opportunity cost by not attracting the right talent to my company to fill open positions?

Overall impact to the business

There are some costs that are more easily defined than others, but in today's hectic lifestyles of most employees there is a value to having time off to take care of personal needs. There is an even higher value in having paid time off to take care of needs like mental health, personal care, doctor's appointments, childcare, or elder care.

If you are having trouble conceptualizing the overall cost of employment for your company check out a helpful calculator from CalcXML that will calculate Employee Total Compensation. This calculator is from an employer's point of view so enter your employer's contributions to tax, benefits and insurance.

The benefits of offering contemporary plans

Have you thought about your leave of absence plans? Many companies do not have a plan with regard to leaves of absence. Some employers are not required to have any plans under the federal regulations, but they are required to have them under state statutes.

The largest companies in the world are mindful of their requirements. I'm asking you to do something not all of them do – think about how it impacts your culture.

Maternity leave is usually what we talk about in the U.S. as a primary leave of absence under the FMLA and it's a common request from employees in companies of all sizes. Some employers are not required to follow FMLA (less than 50 employees and other concerns, or if you're not sure, see FMLA Leave at the DOL).

FMLA does not require *payment* to employees when they take a leave of absence. And of course there's controversy about the idea of paid leave versus the protection of your job. This is sometimes a contentious issue for legislators and human rights champions but it's an awfully difficult question for the business owner or HR professional.

How do we manage the necessity for providing someone ample time to care for themselves and their child, preserve their position and ensure the least disruption to the business? Oh and, by the way, keep it as cost minimal as possible? Right. Not easy.

Let's be practical – and it's something you'll notice a progressive employer like Sir Richard Branson is doing at Virgin with a progressive paternity leave policy. He decided to test a leave policy at a sub-set of his companies first. By testing the waters the team at Virgin could analyze the demand, volume of utilization, and cost. This allowed his team to determine two things.

1) Is this a benefit that will be used and valued by employees?
2) Forecast of the cost.

Will this work for you even if you're not a global business like Virgin?

No doubt the team at Virgin projected both of these factors before the test group was initiated. And you should create a forecast too before implementing any benefit. In addition, you should consider whether offering such a benefit is precedent setting or establishes a sense of entitlement. Precedents and entitlements can upset your otherwise positive culture, so proceed with caution!

The evolving workplace

Denver is a beautiful city. It has many things to offer – the Rockies (mountains and baseball), the Broncos, rolling plains, great skiing, hiking, fishing, and... yes... weed. You can stroll along the streets of Lower Downtown (LoDo, if you're in the know) and smell the sweet nectar of marijuana pouring out of any number of establishments. There is an economic boom in Denver and other parts of Colorado including a newly found niche tourism industry completely based around legalized marijuana.

Whether you're into weed for alternative medicinal reasons, you like to catch a buzz now and again, or you hate it all together – weed is here to stay and it's an example of a modern-day evolution of our workplace. In the 1990s we had Internet and in the early 2000s we had mobile devices. In the near future we will confront the legalization of recreational drugs.

What's an employer to do?

States differ from one to another on how an employer can enforce its own regulations, and quite frankly you can be left somewhat dazed and confused if you try to navigate through each state law. Whether you're an employer or an employee here are some good rules of thumb.

This seems obvious, but if you operate in a state that has not recognized marijuana as a legal drug then you don't have to tolerate it in your workplace. You can screen for it just as you always have. But if you don't have a policy on drug screening, now would be a good time to consider implementing one.

Feel confident in saying, "But it's not legal here" to any employee or candidate who fails a drug screening following a cannabis vacation.

Do *not* target people for drug screenings following a cannabis vacation. Targeted drug screenings are not random. Don't put yourself in jeopardy because you suspect someone will fail a drug test. If you truly have a random drug screening program and someone is truly included on a random basis then you're fine. If someone is behaving in an unsafe manor or smoking on company property during work hours (and that's not permitted per your policies) then a drug screening may be warranted.

If you operate in a state that has legalized marijuana in general and an employee does not have a prescription need for medicinal purposes, you're likely able to administer drug testing as you always did. This is considered "off-duty" usage. Read more about *Coats v. Dish Network*.

What are the job requirements for the position? If the position has a high risk for safety you should look at legal marijuana similarly as you do any other prescription drug under your safety and ADA compliance practices.

If an employee is prescribed the use of marijuana for medicinal purposes, remember that the use of the drug will be covered by HIPAA's protected health information provisions. Refrain from speaking openly about someone's use, need for the drug, behaviors, etc.

With legalization differing from state to state there are even more pitfalls in terminating an employee due to drug use. Make sure you follow the interactive process under the ADA if your state's statute requires it.

Weed in the workplace is one example of the evolution of the workplace you'll experience during the time of business ownership. Take your time in thinking through how you will adjust to the changing laws. Seek advice of counsel if need be. A few hundred dollars in advice fees from an attorney could keep you out of the $250,000 problems other employers have faced!

Conclusion

HR can be simple. I promise you it can be.

For a long time the human resources professional has focused on compliance and rules and regulations. It felt like a demonstrative part of business because quite frankly it was. But slowly we are realizing that rules and compliance aren't as essential if we hire the best people and engage them effectively. You don't have to run a multi-million dollar company to attract top talent and reward them favorably for their contributions. You don't have to create complicated performance management programs and analyze data for months before turning around a report that shows your team is under performing.

Stop the madness with all of that!

The reason I started the book with guides on hiring top talent is I believe it's truly the first step in having a successful business. If you surround yourself with the best people for the job they will lead the company in the right direction. If you allow these people to be empowered and recognize their achievements you won't have an issue with getting the most out of their talents. They will naturally want to give you more.

Engagement is a powerful thing that companies are just starting to investigate and implement effectively. As I mentioned in that section of the book I also think engagement is unique to each business. There's no one-size-fits-all magic pill you can take to start engaging your team. You might try something that works well. You might try something that falls flat. Don't be discouraged by that. Keep plugging away at the 12 steps I outlined for you in the Engage section of the book. One thing at a time. Simple changes. Big impact.

Successful businesses don't happen overnight. It takes practice and it takes dedication. You've clearly made the decision to have a strong business. You're interested in growing and thriving in your industry. The level of effort you take to develop sales and marketing programs, or the care you take in determining the appropriate vendor and supply chain for your business, is the same level of diligence you should exercise with the people in your company. Don't let your uncertainty about human resources result in neglecting this part of your business. Your team deserves better. And so do you.

I sincerely hope this book has been a helpful introduction to simple and effective tactics you can take to improve the human resources aspects of your business. Don't forget to visit OperamHR.com/book for more tools, tactics and guides!

Suggested Reading

Recruit

The top two search engines – Indeed and Simply Hired – accounted for the bulk of online recruiting activity in 2016. More from the experts at HRDive.com and Silkroad:
http://www.hrdive.com/news/indeed-simplyhired-lead-the-online-job-search-engine-race/418139/

Why is HR the marketing team's new best friend? Check it out via Ad Age's article: "CMOs, Meet Your New Best Friend: The CHRO"
http://adage.com/article/agency-viewpoint/cmos-meet-friend-chro/299979/

Do you know what your company's profile looks like on Indeed.com? Here's a link to check it out!
https://www.indeed.com/Best-Places-to-Work?attributionid=footer

ENGAGE

Zappos is often credited with impeccable corporate culture and engagement. Here's a take from Quartz.com "Holacracy at Zappos: It's either the future of management or a social experiment gone awry." http://qz.com/317918/holacracy-at-zappos-its-either-the-future-of-management-or-a-social-experiment-gone-awry/

Being there is a core concept of engagement. Don't take my word for it! Check out the concept from the experts at Wharton School of Business: http://executiveeducation.wharton.upenn.edu/thought-leadership/wharton-at-work/2014/11/being-there

Challenge your thoughts about the standard work day. Could you make adjustments to the norm? Check out a few company's experiments via The Atlantic online:
http://www.theatlantic.com/business/archive/2015/06/four-day-workweek/396530/?utm_source=SFTwitter

Fridays are not even a workday at a company called Treehouse. Would that work for you? Check it out via Washington Post online:
https://www.washingtonpost.com/local/at-some-start-ups-fridays-are-so-casual-everyone-can-stay-home/2015/02/06/31e8407e-9d1c-11e4-96cc-e858eba91ced_story.html?utm_term=.69edb08dd3ea

40-hour work weeks should be the norm, not the exception. Here's why via The Wall Street Journal online:
https://www.wsj.com/articles/radical-idea-at-the-office-a-40-hour-workweek-1444754956?mod=e2fb

When we have to write articles counseling employees on erasing the guilt of vacation time, we know we have an issue in the US. Check out this blog from August 2016 on Huffington Post "How to Stop Worrying About the Consequences and Take Vacation":
http://m.huffpost.com/us/entry/7983686?ncid=tweetlnkushpmg00000034

Beyond salary, employees want more paid time off – and you're probably not surprised! From Society of Human Resources Management:
http://www.shrm.org/hrdisciplines/benefits/articles/pages/employees-value-pto.aspx

Sir Richard Branson is a progressive leader and thinker and he's making paternity leave part of his corporate culture. He tested it first and then implemented. Good strategy! Read out it via Forbes online:
https://www.forbes.com/forbes/welcome/?toURL=https://www.forbes.com/sites/susanadams/2015/06/12/virgins-new-paternity-leave-policy-is-it-worth-the-hype/&refURL=https://www.google.com/&referrer=https://www.google.com/

Kevin Kruse is an engagement guru and New York Times best-selling author. Read about his engagement strategies online:
www.KevinKruse.com

COMPLY

The most significant co-employment litigation in modern times was the $97 Million assessment to Microsoft. Here's an article that ran on LA Times online in 2000 to help you understand the issues in this groundbreaking case: "Microsoft to Pay $97 Million to End Temp Worker Lawsuit"
http://articles.latimes.com/2000/dec/13/business/fi-64817

Modern day and extremely public issues of corporate distrust, discrimination and harassment. Look no further than the debacles that plagued Fox News in 2016. via CNN Online:

http://money.cnn.com/2016/09/06/media/gretchen-carlson-fox-news-lawsuit-settled/

One of the best overviews of overtime rules via the source, the Department of Labor:
https://www.dol.gov/whd/overtime/fs17a_overview.pdf

Do you understand the concept of Highly Compensated Individuals? Here is a great explanation via the Department of Labor: https://www.dol.gov/whd/overtime/fs17h_highly_comp.pdf

Tracking employee's overtime is complicated. Here are the reasons you need to do it via Fortune Magazine:
http://fortune.stfi.re/2016/07/22/managers-track-employee-overtime-hours/?sf=xrjvler

You may have heard about the concept of equal pay but do you know the modern federal case that brought the most significant changes to us? Learn about Lilly Ledbetter and the groundbreaking case via this publication from the EEOC:
https://www.eeoc.gov/eeoc/publications/brochure-equal_pay_and_ledbetter_act.cfm

Discrimination cases are based on protected classes. Get to know the types of discrimination the EEOC aggressively protects:
https://www.eeoc.gov/laws/types/

The Office of Federal Contract Compliance Programs or OFCCP provides oversight to government contractors. But their guidance could have impact on all employers in the US. Read their position on the value and necessity of pay transparency:
https://www.dol.gov/ofccp/PayTransparency.html

Do you know your rights and obligations under USERRA? USERRA stands for Uniformed Services Employment and Reemployment Rights Act and assists veterans in employment eligibility.
http://www.dol.gov/elaws/userra.htm

Earned sick time could be a federal issue, not just a state-specific issue. The OFCCP and NLRB have issued recommendations on the issue and Massachusetts has implemented regulations as have other states. Here is a summary from the Massachusetts Attorney General: http://www.mass.gov/ago/doing-business-in-massachusetts/workplace-rights/leave-time/earned-sick-time.html And paid sick leave from the "country" of California:

http://www.dir.ca.gov/dlse/Paid_Sick_Leave.htm

Do you understand Family Medical Leave Act and if you even need to comply? Check out the federal guidelines – but don't forget to look up your state's guidance on this topic! It can differ from the federal statute. http://www.dol.gov/whd/fmla/

Just because marijuana is legal in your personal life doesn't mean that they can be impaired when at the workplace. This is an ever changing part of our business life. Read more from The Washington Post: https://www.washingtonpost.com/news/post-nation/wp/2015/06/15/colorado-supreme-court-says-companies-can-fire-workers-for-using-medical-marijuana-in-their-off-hours/?utm_term=.a98ed30b9af4

About the Author

 **Amanda King** is the Founder and President of Operam HR. She provides human resources management, consulting, and human resources training to businesses in growth mode, striving to help business owners develop a solid foundation and business strategy so they can be successful. She works to improve a company's bottom line by solidifying organization structure, company culture and employee relations.

Amanda is a passionate people advocate. Her goal is to create solutions to issues and challenges of modern business and employee needs. Her experience with large, multi-national corporations taught her the importance of balancing the needs of management and employees through education, open lines of communication, and a willingness to evolve employee programs as the needs of the workforce change.

Amanda was educated at esteemed institutions like George Mason University in Virginia where she received her bachelor's degree, Oxford University in the UK, and Cornell University in New York where she received her Masters Certificate in Human Resources Management. She's worked for global organizations like Spectris plc, Ahold USA, and Harsco Corporation.

Capabilities and frequently completed services for clients:

- Compliance
  - Employee handbook
  - HR policy manuals
  - Audits of personnel files and various HR processes

- Training
  - o Anti-discrimination and anti-harassment training
  - o HIPAA compliance
  - o Employee engagement strategies
  - o Management skills training

- Talent management
  - o Sourcing and screening top talent
  - o Objective interview and evaluation tools

Blog content of interest:

www.OperamHR.com/about;
www.OperamHR.com/category/engagement/

Contact the Author:

Amanda King, SPHR
Operam HR
257 E. Market St, 2nd floor
York, PA 17403

+1 (717) 659-0247
Amanda@OperamHR.com
www.OperamHR.com

www.Facebook.com/OperamHR
www.Twitter.com/OperamHR
www.LinkedIn.com/in/AmandaKing
https://www.linkedin.com/company-beta/18010735/

Made in the USA
Middletown, DE
06 January 2018